MACMILLAN MODERN DRAMATISTS

Macmillan Modern Dramatists
Series Editors: Bruce and Adele King

Published titles

Further titles in preparation

MACMILLAN MODERN DRAMATISTS

BERTOLT BRECHT

Ronald Speirs

First published 1987

Published by
Higher and Further Education Division
MACMILLAN PUBLISHERS LTD
Houndmills, Basingstoke, Hampshire RG21 2XS
and London
Companies and representatives
throughout the world

Typeset by Wessex Typesetters
(Division of The Eastern Press Ltd)
Frome, Somerset

Printed in Hong Kong

British Library Cataloguing in Publication Data
Speirs, Ronald
Bertolt Brecht. – (Macmillan modern dramatists)
1. Brecht, Bertolt – Criticism and
interpretation
I. Title
832'.912   PT2603.R397Z/
ISBN 0–333–29206–5
ISBN 0–333–29207–3 (pbk)

Contents

List of Plates

Acknowledgments

The author and publishers wish to thank the following who have kindly given permission for the use of copyright material:

Associated Book Publishers (U.K.) Ltd., the author and translators for extracts from various plays, poems and diaries by Bertolt Brecht, Methuen, London.

The Bertolt Brecht Erben for extracts from unpublished material in the keeping of the Bertolt Brecht archives.

Frau Gerda Goedhart and Frau Vera Tenschert of the Berliner Ensemble for photographs from Ensemble productions.

Every effort has been made to trace all the copyright holders but if any have been inadvertently overlooked the publishers will be pleased to make the necessary arrangement at the first opportunity.

The copyright in any previously unpublished translations of work by Bertolt Brecht belongs to Stefan S. Brecht.

Preface

Nobody can sit down to write a book about Brecht today without being keenly aware of the many other books that have already been written on the subject. Even if the reader of this volume has not yet read much by or about Brecht, he is very likely to have heard the terms 'Epic Theatre' or 'alienation effect', and be aware that Brecht is generally thought of as a writer who addresses his work to the heads rather than the hearts of his audience. This opposition reason-feeling is now so firmly entrenched in the minds of many school-leavers coming up to university that they find difficulty in even recognising the part being played by their emotions as they read or watch a performance of a Brechtian play. The object of this book is not, of course, to deny the role of the intellect in Brecht's writing, but rather to help correct the balance in the understanding of the effects actually produced by his plays.

Much of the background work on this book was done at the Bertolt Brecht Archive of the 'Akademie der Künste der DDR', where I was made very welcome and given great

Preface

assistance by Frau Berger, Frau Kuntze, Dr Seidel, Dr Glaeser and Dr Braun, for which I should now like to thank them. I must also thank the British Council, the Ministry of Culture of the GDR, and the University of Birmingham for making possible a lengthy period of study in Berlin. I am grateful to Professor John Fuegi of the University of Maryland for permission to read in manuscript his study of Brecht's work as a director, shortly to be published by Cambridge University Press. Thanks are due also to many colleagues in the Arts Faculty of Birmingham University for support and debate, particularly to Dr Michael Butler, and to Mrs Catherine Tooze and Mrs Christine Marlowe for typing the manuscript.

Editions, Translations, Abbreviations

As far as possible I have quoted from the Eyre Methuen translation of Brecht's collected works, edited by John Willett and Ralph Manheim. Because this edition is not yet complete it has been necessary also to quote from other translations or directly from the original German, supplying my own translations. For ease of reference the source of a quotation is generally given in brackets in the body of the text, using the following abbreviations throughout:

I
2i   Volume of the collected plays
2ii etc   in the Eyre Methuen edition

Aj   *Arbeitsjournal (1938–55)*
BBA   Material from the Bertolt Brecht Archive
BT   *Brecht on Theatre*
CM   *Brechts 'Mutter Courage und ihre Kinder': Materialien* (1982)

Editions, Translations, Abbreviations

D   *Diaries 1920–1922* (trans. J. Willett)
GM   *Brechts 'Leben des Galilei': Materialien* (1981)
GW   *Gesammelte Werke* (20 vols)
KM   *Brechts 'Kaukasischer Kreidekreis': Materialien* (1985)
P   *Poems* (ed. Willett and Manheim)
SJ   *Saint Joan of the Stockyards* (trans. Frank Jones)
SM   *Brechts 'Guter Mensch von Sezuan': Materialien* (1982)
T   *Tagebücher 1920–1922. Autobiographische Aufzeichnungen 1920–1954*

Editors' Preface

The *Macmillan Modern Dramatists* is an international series of introductions to major and significant nineteenth- and twentieth-century dramatists, movements and new forms of drama in Europe, Great Britain, America and new nations such as Nigeria and Trinidad. Besides new studies of great and influential dramatists of the past, the series includes volumes on contemporary authors, recent trends in the theatre and on many dramatists, such as writers of farce, who have created theatre 'classics' while being neglected by literary criticism. The volumes in the series devoted to individual dramatists include a biography, a survey of the plays, and detailed analysis of the most significant plays, along with discussion, where relevant, of the political, social, historical and theatrical context. The authors of the volumes, who are involved with theatre as playwrights, directors, actors, teachers and critics, are concerned with the plays as theatre and discuss such matters as performance, character interpretation and staging, along with themes and contexts.

BRUCE KING
ADELE KING

1
Introduction: Life and Works

To begin at the end: Brecht died on 14 August 1956 in East Berlin. One of his best-known poems anticipates his death:

> I need no gravestone, but
> If you need one for me
> I would like it to bear these words:
> He made suggestions. We
> Carried them out.
> Such an inscription would
> Honour us all.
>   (P. 218)

In contrast to the self-effacing persona projected in this poem, Brecht ensured that by the time of his death his name was known world-wide, numbering among that relatively small group of modern authors, including Shaw, Orwell and Kafka, whose names survive in adjectival form. 'Brechtian' or 'brechtisch' is an established part of cultural vocabulary, referring not only to a method of staging plays, but also to a style of expression, a way of thinking, a way of looking at the world even. Nor was this a case of a modest man having greatness thrust upon him. As a young man Brecht had ambitions to prove that he was the 'German Shakespeare', and had set out in the 1920s quite deliberately to conquer the theatrical centre of the Weimar Republic, Berlin. So far was he in those days from being self-effacing that, when he heard that the coveted Kleist Prize for the most promising young playwright might be awarded *jointly* to himself and his close friend, Arnolt Bronnen, he let it be known that he would not accept nomination on those terms. The gambit was successful: the Kleist Prize was awarded to Brecht alone. For a man who later liked to present himself as one who made 'suggestions', Brecht showed a remarkable talent throughout his life for getting such suggestions accepted.

In his writing, as in his life, Brecht was a man of the will. In about 1926 he wrote of politics: 'Politics, too, are only any good if sufficient ideas are available (. . .), the triumph over humanity. To be able to do the right thing, ruthlessly, with severity' (GW 20, 15). In later life, despite a liking for the habitus of a gentle, oriental sage, Brecht still took a hard line on politics, remarking about the Soviet imposition of Communism on the Germans in the Russian-occupied sector: 'Better to have socialism by dictate than no socialism at all.' (Aj, 864) (having ensured, incidentally, a degree of personal liberty for himself that he was willing to deny to others).

In contrast to, say, Keats's definition of the poet's mind as one distinguished by its chameleon-like 'negative capability', Brecht's imagination, too, was strongly influenced by his wilful character. He once observed in his diary, for example, that his memory operated actively on the information it stored: 'In one way I am better off than others, particularly as far as memories are concerned; for my brain orders material with the help of aesthetic devices, so that I see more beautiful and more significant images than other people. Admittedly, I appear to have a worse memory than many people I know.' (T, 228) Fortunately for his writing, Brecht's characteristic will to master life imaginatively was balanced by an underlying awareness of the resistance of life to such attempts at mastery. Much of his best work is informed by a tension between his sense of the way life is and his sense of how it could or should be.

The concepts, such as 'Epic Theatre' and the 'alienation device' with which his name is now so firmly associated, however, reflect the active, wilful character of his imagination and outlook on the world. Epic Theatre was conceived by Brecht as one that would imitate the doings of men in such a way that it would put the spectators in a position to form a judgement about what they saw on the stage, a judgement upon which they might then act in the world outside the theatre. The alienation device was the central means of achieving that end, for it was intended to present the all too familiar world in an 'estranging' or 'defamiliarising' manner, so that the audience is made to *see* the things they look at, unseeing, every day. In order to facilitate such active seeing on the part of the spectator, the imagination of the writer must previously have worked actively on the material of experience; hence the alienation device.

The ancient image of life as a journey proved to be more than a metaphor in Brecht's experience. True, he spent his last years, as he had spent his youth, in Germany. But the route he took from Augsburg to Berlin was a circuitous one, and the Germany into which he was born a very different country from the one in which he died. His grave, in the old Huguenot 'Dorotheenfriedhof', lies in what is now East Berlin, administrative capital of the German Democratic Republic (GDR), a country thrice removed in political terms from the 'Second German Empire' of Wilhelm II in which the young Brecht grew up. The creation of that Empire in 1871, following the defeat of France by Prussia, had fulfilled an old German dream of national unification and greatness. It was a dream that turned into a nightmare during the First World War when the ambition to be the equal, or more, of the older European nations ended in defeat, partial occupation (by the hated French yet again), and the humiliating treaty of Versailles – a location symbolically chosen by the victors to echo the Prussian humiliation of France in 1871. The 'revolution' that accompanied the end of the war resulted, not in the seizure of power by the proletariat or the Bolsheviks, but in the establishment of parliamentary democracy. This new creation, the Weimar Republic, sadly enjoyed too little support from the population, and came to an end after only fifteen years when the National Socialists under Hitler came to power and immediately proceeded to make that power total. The GDR in which Brecht settled after the defeat of Hitler in the Second World War was one of two simultaneous new beginnings for the Germans after the catastrophe of Nazism, the other being the Federal Republic of Germany. The journey of Brecht's life was closely bound up with the erratic historical course of his country.

Brecht, christened Eugen Berthold, was born in Augsburg in Southern Germany in 1898, the oldest son of Berthold Friedrich Brecht, who became managing director of Haindl's paper factory just two years after the birth of his son. The young Brecht's wilful character evidently began to show itself at an early age according to childhood play-mates who recall that games had to be organized according to his wishes, and that he did not mind showing that he was the boss's son in order to get his own way.[1] In later life, too, his friends, lovers and collaborators had similar experiences.[2]

Brecht's literary interests and ambitions also emerged fairly early, for, when still a schoolboy of fifteen, he founded a school literary magazine entitled *The Harvest* (*Die Ernte*), publishing in it some of his first poems, literary essays and a one-act play entitled *The Bible* (*Die Bibel*).[3] This limited outlet cannot have satisfied his desire to appear in print, for at the outbreak of war in 1914 he seized the opportunity to write a series of 'Augsburg War Letters' for one of the local newspapers. These juvenilia, a mixture of verse and prose, were not generally known about until after Brecht's death. Had they been reprinted during his lifetime, even his considerable talent for 'covering his tracks'[4] would have been sorely put to the test, for, without being crudely jingoistic, they are imbued with an idealistic enthusiasm for the 'holy' German imperial cause, acknow-ledging and affirming that the sacrifices it demanded were necessary.

The style and content of these early pieces would have embarrassed the anarchic, but generally apolitical, bohe-mian he became in the twenties and, even more so, the later poet of the Communist revolution. Nevertheless, there is a certain continuity underlying his transformation from propagandist of imperialism via anarchic, cynical vitalist into propagandist of communism.[5] His support of the German war effort in 1914 evidently satisfied a set of emotional, ethical and imaginative needs, which included the feeling of being at one with the community at large, being involved in events of world historical significance, a respect for sacrifice, dedication to a high, even 'holy' ideal, and imaginative participation in acts of violence and suffering.

As the war proceeded, Brecht lost his initial illusions about its ideal character. He was almost expelled from school for failing to deliver the expected trite essay on the theme *dulce et decorum est pro patria mori*. Indeed his reaction to that loss of illusion was so strong that it carried him to the opposite extreme of cynical, apolitical, individualistic sensualism; to an inverted version of his original set of values which, even as it denied the value of idealism, confirmed that his own idealistic streak was still strong. This tendency in him then reasserted itself in something very close to its original form when, in 1929, at a time of intensifying *class*-war – which even took the form of pitched battles between communists and fascists on the streets of Berlin – Brecht again felt that he had a cause to which he could and should commit himself and his writing. His allegiance was now to the Communist revolution, but (allowing for the obvious differences, particularly a new insistence on the rationality of the enterprise) many of the values that that commitment entailed were the same as those that had aroused his enthusiasm in 1914. In all three phases of his development one can detect the same celebration of the power of the will: firstly, the will of the nation to purify itself and prove its '*Größe*' ('greatness'); then the will of the exceptional, even 'pathological' individual to live a life untrammelled by the demands of others; and lastly, the will of the revolutionary proletariat to make the world 'habitable'.

At the end of 1917 Brecht moved from Augsburg to nearby Munich to register as a medical student at the University, thereby postponing the possibility of call-up, and also gaining new opportunities and leisure to pursue his literary interests. In 1918 he had the distinction of being ejected from a seminar run by the professor of theatre studies, Artur Kutscher, for attacking the work of the latter's latest protégé, the Expressionist (and later Nazi) Hanns Johst, whose play, *The Lonely One* (*Der Einsame*), prompted, by way of a counter-blast, Brecht's own first full-length play, *Baal* (begun 1918, completed 1920).

Between 1918 and 1924 Brecht's life was mainly based in Munich, though he made a number of sorties, some of them fairly extended, to Berlin, where he hoped to establish his literary and theatrical career. During these years he completed, apart from *Baal*, two plays entitled *Drums in the Night* (*Trommeln in der Nacht*) (1919–22) and *In the Jungle* (*Im Dickicht*) (1923), and a collection of very effective lyrical poems of blasphemous intent, under the title *Hauspostille* (*Devotions*). *Drums in the Night* had its premiere at the Kammerspiele in Munich in the autumn of 1922, but was soon moved to the Deutsches Theater in Berlin at the end of that year, where it became one of the most popular plays of the season. Brecht did not enjoy any similar success with audiences again until 1928, when *The Threepenny Opera* (*Die Dreigroschenoper*) was staged at the Theater am Schiffbauerdamm (the later home of the Berliner Ensemble), and became – thanks in good measure to Kurt Weill's bitter-sweet music and a cast of professionals from the popular stage – one of the greatest theatrical hits of the Weimar Republic. Brecht's and Weill's attempt to cash in on its success by repeating the formula in *Happy End* (based on a libretto by Brecht's assistant, Elisabeth Hauptmann), was a dismal failure. They did not fare much better with their next collaboration either; the much more ambitious project of a full-scale opera – *Rise and Fall of the City of Mahagonny* (*Aufstieg und Fall der Stadt Mahagonny*); fortunately, this lively and imaginative account of the dreams and disappointments inspired by life in modern cities has subsequently gained the place it deserves in the modern operatic repertoire.

Mahagonny, completed in 1929, offered no cure for the sickness it diagnosed. Later that year, however, Brecht's writing changed profoundly. Under the impact of the worsening political situation and as a result of his studies (he had begun to read Marx's *Das Kapital* as early as 1926), he began to write plays designed to promote collective, revolutionary action to eradicate the social and economic causes of human suffering. The first completed works written with this aim in mind were some short pieces that Brecht classified as *Lehrstücke*, meaning teaching or rather 'learning' plays. The idea was to side-step bourgeois commercial theatre by providing playlets that could be studied and performed by groups of users – such as schoolchildren, or workers' choral organisations – with needs that Brecht thought could not be satisfied by simply watching plays in the normal type of theatre. In place of a 'theatre for consumers', Brecht wanted to create a 'theatre for those who produce it' (*Theater für die Produzenten*), one where the value of a production would lie in the preparation and performance of the play rather than in watching it. In principle, plays of this type did not need to be performed before an audience at all, but if one were present it should be drawn into some form of active participation – as in the *Baden-Baden Cantata* (*Das Badener Lehrstück vom Einverständnis*) (1929) – where the 'crowd' is supplied with responses to make to questions asked of them, and instructed in the correct way to analyse and deal with an ethical–social problem.

Other plays of this type, such as *He who said Yes* (*Der Jasager*), *The Decision* (*Die Maßnahme*) or *The Exception and the Rule* (*Die Ausnahme und die Regel*) (all 1929/30) were written with the needs of a quite small group of performers in mind, who would acquire or practise dialectical thinking by close study of the play text, *and* by its enactment; in the sense that they would learn to understand, through the presentation of character and behaviour, that social interaction is a matter of mutual shaping, limitation, and development, i.e. a dialectical process. Well-meaning though the rationalist–educative intentions underlining these experiments were, they produced some unexpected and unwelcome results. The first version of *He who said Yes*, for example, was welcomed by some right-wing reviewers, while *The Decision*, which ends with the execution of an inexperienced, and therefore dangerous young revolutionary in China by more experienced comrades, elicited such a hostile response from official Communist circles that Brecht felt he had to put a ban on future performances. To this day it has not been performed in the GDR.

Brecht's experiments with the *Lehrstück* did not mean that he had abandoned all interest in writing full-length plays for the professional theatre. Rather, his aim was now to use it as a platform for the political education of the audience through such plays as *Saint Joan of the Stockyards* (*Die heilige Johanna der Schlachthöfe*) and *The Mother*, both completed in 1931. In attempting to use the theatre – despite its assumed subservience to bourgeois needs and interests – as a means of confronting the audience with unpalatable facts about society, Brecht was, of course, doing nothing particularly new in the history of German drama. In the eighteenth century the young Friedrich Schiller, before he became subject to 'refining' influences at the court of Weimar, had railed against the age, giving his first play, *The Robbers* (*Die Räuber*), the motto '*in tyrannos*'.

Closer to Brecht's time, the Expressionists, shocked by the First World War, had used the stage for direct appeals to the conscience or soul of the audience, while Erwin Piscator had made several attempts during the Twenties to establish an overtly political theatre in Germany, his enterprises often being funded by members of the very class of capitalists whose domination he was bent on destroying.[7] However, these two new plays by Brecht offered a sufficiently disturbing challenge to the political order of the late Weimar Republic not to receive public performances on the live stage when they were ready: even for a 'closed' performance before an invited audience, *The Mother* (*Die Mutter*) was only permitted to be read rather than enacted, while *Saint Joan*, or part of it, was given just one performance as a radio play. Even such limited possibilities as these, however, disappeared completely in 1933, when the National Socialists, under the leadership of Adolf Hitler, came to power. On 28 February of that year, on the day after the burning of the *Reichstag*, Brecht left Germany to go into voluntary 'exile'.[8]

Brecht's travels in exile – 'changing countries oftener than our shoes' (P, 320) – took him ever further from Germany: from Autumn 1933 until April 1939 he was based in Denmark; from May 1939 till April 1940 in Sweden; From April 1940 till May 1941 in Finland; from Helsinki he travelled via Leningrad, Moscow and Vladivostok to America, where he lived from 1941 till 1947 in Santa Monica, Southern California. While in exile, particularly in the mid-1930s, Brecht considered that the struggle against fascism had first claim on his time. He immediately saw the need to draw other exiled intellectuals – not only communists – into a 'united front' against fascism, but he caused embarrassment to those organising the official Communist United Front policy by delivering a speech at the 'First

International Writers' Congress for the Defence of Culture' in Paris in 1935, in which he argued that the struggle against the 'barbarism' of fascism could only be successful if it were also a struggle against the capitalist system in which it was rooted. Brecht wrote another speech, repeating the same arguments, for the second of these congresses in 1937, but was unable to deliver it because the organisers, to his surprise and indignation, did not send him an invitation to attend until four days before it was due to take place!

As part of his anti-fascist work Brecht accepted, after some hesitation, the co-editorship of the Moscow-based journal *The Word* (*Das Wort*). Here again, however, his experiences with the communists in Moscow were not entirely happy ones. Although they wanted to have his name as one of the editors, his editorial judgements on a number of important issues were simply not respected. He also had considerable difficulties with another journal published in Moscow, *International Literature* (*Internationale Literatur*), which not only failed to pay him for certain contributions, but provided a platform for Georg Lukacs, and those associated with him, to attack Brecht's work. Repeatedly during his career as a communist writer Brecht was to find himself in conflict with these exponents of the conservative aesthetic doctrine of 'Socialist Realism'.[9]

A number of the plays Brecht wrote in exile were devoted principally to the struggle against fascism. Like his speeches and essays, they seek to demonstrate that the roots of this particular evil lay in the economic crisis of late capitalism and in the class-conflicts that became intensified as a result of that crisis. *Round Heads and Pointed Heads* (*Die Rundköpfe und die Spitzköpfe*) (first version, 1932), a parable play based on Shakespeare's *Measure for Measure*,

11

claimed that the racist ideology of the Nazis was merely a diversionary tactic to obscure the fact that the most important conflict in society was not between the races but between the exploiters and the exploited. *The Resistible Rise of Arturo Ui* (*Der aufhaltsame Aufstieg des Arturo Ui*) (1941), too, sought to show the links between the interests of big business and the accession to power of Hitler. Alongside these caricaturing parables, however, Brecht was willing to employ other, more traditional forms if he thought they served the needs of the hour. His *Fear and Misery of the Third Reich* (*Furcht und Elend des Dritten Reiches*) (1937–8), for example, was composed of realistic, in some cases almost naturalistic, thumb-nail sketches of life under fascism, while *Señora Carrar's Rifles* (*Die Gewehre der Frau Carrar*), written in 1937 to enlist support for the Left against the Spanish fascists under Franco, comes surprisingly close to the type of Aristotelian play, with linear plot and rising emotional tension, favoured by the proponents of Socialist Realism; ironically enough, although regarded by Brecht as an opportunistic play, designed to meet the demands of a particular situation, it is still one of the most frequently produced of his plays in the GDR.

Whereas Brecht's more directly anti-fascist plays now tend to seem dated, others of his plays written in exile, some of which were orginally conceived as anti-fascist pieces, have survived to become the 'classics' of the Brechtian repertoire: *The Life of Galileo* (*Leben des Galilei*) (first version, 1938) *Mother Courage and her Children* (*Mutter Courage und ihre Kinder*) (1939), *The Good Person of Szechwan* (*Der gute Mensch von Sezuan*) (1939–41), *Mr Puntila and his Man Matti* (*Herr Puntila und sein Knecht Matti*) (1941) and *The Caucasian Chalk Circle* (*Der Kaukasische Kreidekreis*) (1944). Despite some of his programmatic statements about the reduced importance of the individual in the modern world, and in the modern drama, Brecht, when surveying his production, would list the succession of memorable *characters* around which he had built these plays.

After being required to testify before the Committee on Un-American Activities in 1947, Brecht, who all along had been unhappy with life in capitalist America (though he did at least survive to criticise it, unlike many German socialists and communists who had sought asylum from Hitler in Stalin's Russia), decided to return to Europe. He went in the first instance to Switzerland where there was another large colony of German exiles. There he was able, having been deprived for fifteen years of any such opportunity, to collaborate on a stage production in German, with German-speaking actors and for a German-speaking audience, and thus to put to the acid test of theatrical practice theories that still largely only existed on paper. Helene Weigel also needed, after a long absence from the stage, to discover whether she could still act. The location chosen for the experiment was the small Swiss provincial town of Chur, where Brecht, collaborating with the designer Caspar Neher, staged an adaptation of Sophocles' *Antigone* (1948).

Brecht regarded Switzerland as merely another temporary resting place where he could make plans to settle more permanently elsewhere. He conducted negotiations simultaneously, and secretly, with both Austria and the GDR, proposing in the one case to re-establish the Salzburg Theatre Festival, while discussing in East Germany the establishment of a new theatrical company. As a result he acquired both Austrian citizenship, which guaranteed him the great benefit of freedom of movement, and his 'own' theatre company in East Berlin, the Berliner Ensemble, which was actually to be managed by Helene Weigel (Brecht did not even sign a permanent contract with the company). They moved to Berlin in 1948, settling there in 1949.

As far as the finances of the Ensemble were concerned, Brecht's work was generously supported by the authorities in Berlin, so that he was able, for example, to spend up to nine months rehearsing a single production; thereafter, admittedly, plays tended to stay in the repertoire for years. However, the Ensemble was not initially given its own theatre, but had the status of a guest company at the Deutsches Theater under Langhoff (which almost inevitably produced frictions), and spent a good deal of time touring. Brecht also had a number of clashes on aesthetic and ideological matters with the authorities, his work being charged repeatedly with the serious defect of supposed 'formalism'. Nor did his refusal to be 'awed' by the classics, whose works (for example, Goethe's *Urfaust*) were performed in new, boldly critical adaptations by the Ensemble, go down well with cultural functionaries bent on establishing the GDR's claim to be the legitimate and respectful heir of the 'great humanist tradition'. Eventually, however, the company moved into the renovated Theater am Schiffbauerdamm in March 1954. The date of the move seems significant, in that it follows so closely on the scandal in which Brecht became involved concerning the Berlin uprising of 17 June, 1953. On hearing about the events Brecht had written a letter to Walther Ulbricht expressing solidarity with the government, but also urging that there be urgent discussions with the workers about their demands. The official newspaper *Neues Deutschland* published only part of the text, so that it appeared to be a telegram of unqualified support. Although the full text of the letter was subsequently published, Brecht's reputation was so damaged in the West that there ensued a widescale boycott of his plays, and for a number of years it took a brave producer indeed to stage a production of a Brecht play in a West German theatre. Thus, for a time at least, Brecht's hope that Austrian citizenship would ensure that he would not be regarded as 'dead' in one or other of the two Germanies was disappointed. Brecht's period of greatest popularity in *both* Germanies only occurred after this 'uncomfortable' writer was safely dead and buried.

2
The Plays of the Twenties

Brecht is generally known nowadays as a writer and producer of rather demanding political theatre. Yet he enjoyed his greatest popular success in 1928 with *The Threepenny Opera*, a comic ballad opera with unforgettable music by Kurt Weill that has become one of the landmarks of the 'Roaring' or 'Golden' Twenties. Despite Brecht's later efforts to turn it into one, *The Threepenny Opera*, like most of Brecht's plays of the Twenties, is not a work with a clear social or political message. Yet it does contain a good number of the elements of Epic Theatre. In its origins Epic Theatre was something personal – as the sociologist, Fritz Sternberg, once wrote to Brecht: 'Epic Theatre, that's you, my dear Mr Brecht.'[1] At the same time it was something that evolved in interaction with the lively culture of the Weimar Republic, the milieu in which Brecht served his literary apprenticeship. Thus Brecht's work in the 1920s sheds light both on the individual cast of his imagination and on the contemporary influences (if such a word can be applied to an individual in whom the 'spirit of contradiction' was so strongly developed) that fed into his conception of Epic Theatre.

Like the Weimar Republic itself, Brecht's first adult play, *Baal* (first draft, 1918), was in many ways a product of the First World War. Firstly, this 'dramatic biography' of an anarchic poet with an astounding hunger for life was a reaction to the years of multiple deprivation inflicted by the war on the populations of the combatant countries. Although Brecht was fortunate enough to escape service in the field (the nearest he came to it was a short stint as a medical orderly in a military VD clinic), he could not escape his share of the general misery of the war years, while the deaths of so many of his contemporaries from school kept him constantly alive to the war's toll on young lives. Hermann Hesse, whose novella *Klingsor's Last Summer* (*Klingsors letzter Sommer*) (1919) took a similar artist figure for its hero, recalled the mood of the times thus: 'Every one of us had the feeling that he had lost and missed out on something, a piece of life, a piece of the self, a piece of development, adaptation and "savoir vivre".'[2] This generational attitude is also apparent in the welcome given to *Baal* by the artist, Capar Neher, Brecht's close friend and later collaborator, who, after a period of active service, saw in the play a much-needed source of invigoration: 'Your Baal is as good as 10 litres of schnapps.'[3]

In *Baal*, as in Hesse's novella, the imprint of the war is apparent not only in the protagonist's intense appetite for life but also in an all-pervading sense of life's transience, a theme that runs through the whole of Brecht's Twenties work as an abiding mark of the existential shock administered by the war. The unifying action of the seemingly loosely constructed *Baal* is that of a 'dance with death', a medieval form to which the experiences of 1914–18 had given renewed relevance. As his name suggests, Baal is a

17

figure with a mythical dimension: he is (among other things) an embodiment of Eros, the life principle, who is locked in a permanent conflict (that is also an embrace) with Thanatos, the force of death. Death presents itself to Baal in myriad forms – in the shape of corpses, of course, but also in the guise of social conventions and contracts, or in such images of transitoriness as fallen trees, wind-driven clouds, drifting rivers, or the ever-changing but ever-empty skies.

This kind of imagery makes the surface of social relationships transparent, revealing the mythical conflict underlying it, as in the opening scene where Baal is shown in polite society, at a party given in his honour by Mech, a capitalist who would like to publish Baal's poetry. The party ends in disarray after Baal has insulted his would-be patron and blatantly begun to seduce his wife. On one level, Baal's treatment of Mech expresses the anarchic bohemian's revolt against bourgeois convention and capitalist exploitation. Yet the clash of two social types is also a clash between a figure of death and a figure of life. Mech (like Shlink in Brecht's third play, *In the Jungle*) has made his fortune in the timber business: 'Whole forests of cinnamon swim down the rivers of Brasil for my benefit.' (I, 5) Throughout the play (and indeed generally in Brecht's poetry) trees figure as life-symbols, while rivers, by an ancient tradition, represent transience and the force of death. Thus, from the moment Mech introduces himself to Baal, he is presenting himself in the role of Baal's universal antagonist. His party therefore has sinister implications that are hinted at by the words with which he offers Baal food: 'That is the corpse of an eel.' Baal's response to this threat, his seduction of Mech's wife Emily, also has symbolic overtones: faced with the advance of his enemy, death, Baal wrests from its hands an object of beauty and pleasure that he might otherwise have allowed to pass him by.

From this first encounter it can be seen that death is Baal's ally as well as his enemy, for every confrontation with it stimulates him to extend his vital energies and appetites to the full before death claims its eventual victory. Although he will cling to life to the very last, Baal is not concerned with mere survival. Not only does he accept the fact of his own transience, he even accelerates his own destruction in his pursuit of the utmost intensity of experience, an intensity that is purchased by confronting constantly the transitoriness of his existence. Because he is willing to pay the price, Baal achieves the maximum satisfaction from each passing moment. The link between Baal and his young creator was the determination not to be crushed by life. *Baal* came to be written as a fantasy of mastery over life, achieved through a figure whose vitality and ruthlessness enabled him to turn what are normally regarded as sources of pain (such as transience and the related problem of existential isolation) into sources of pleasure and strength; as such, it is a highly characteristic product of Brecht's imagination.

Deprivation and existential shock were not the only war experiences underlying *Baal*. At the outbreak of war the schoolboy Brecht had shown himself to be a patriotic idealist who believed that Germany was right to embark on this 'holy' war. In the course of it his disillusionment carried him to the opposite extreme of distrusting all idealism as a guide to life. He now insisted that ideals were merely ridiculous attempts to erect defences against the harsh realities of life; in the hands of the strong, ideals were a means of exploiting the weak; a task ironically made easier by the need of the weak for ideals to prop up their unsteady lives. *Baal* is a vision of a life lived entirely without the support of any belief in a saving ideal. Baal lives as an animal who 'dies as all animals die', a bundle of appetites, drives and sensations, the seat of an unceasing organic process of consumption and decay, for whom the enjoyment of this process is all the 'meaning' there can be in life. Baal's life is that of the lone wolf who acknowledges no moral obligation to any other creature, seeing others either as threats or as objects of his own desire for pleasure.

As Baal gradually weakens, his victims return to 'haunt' him, but he can still summon up the strength to overcome their threats to his egotism. Johanna, a young girl who drowned herself after being seduced by him, returns in this way, only to be 'consumed' for a second time in his 'Ballad of a Drowned Girl', in which her corpse is made to yield rich poetic effects. Ekart, Baal's homosexual companion whom he knives in a pub-brawl, appears before Baal's delirious eyes when death is very close, but nevertheless Baal manages to crawl past him, out into the open to enjoy a last look at the night sky. The savagery – and intensity – of this vision of life needs to be seen in relation to a war in which the worth of the individual's existence could seem to have been reduced to nothing (the term *Menschenmaterial* – 'human material' – was introduced in the course of it), and in relation to the grand illusions to which Brecht had succumbed at its outset. The cynicism of *Baal* was an act of revenge on the part of an angry, disappointed idealist.

Brecht's rejection of idealism applied not only to the imperialist sentiments fostered in his school days, but also to the revolutionary appeals for self-sacrifice that accompanied the cessation of hostilities – as his next play, *Drums in the Night*, made even plainer. Having once been taken in, it was to be a long time before he felt able to commit himself again to a cause. Generally, the gesture of *Baal* towards its social and cultural context was one of rejection. Baal's name, for example, taken from a Canaanite fertility god whose rites repeatedly seduced the people of Israel away from the worship of Jehovah, signalled Brecht's rejection of the Biblical traditions by which the majority of his compatriots claimed to live. In the narrower literary context of 1918, Brecht's lecherous, drunken and above all *cynical* protagonist represented a calculated affront to the 'messianic', hortatory brand of Expressionism practised by a prominent section of the avant garde at the end of the war. At a time when Expressionists such as Ernst Toller, Franz Werfel or Kurt Hiller were calling for Man's rebirth through the power of the spirit, *Baal* (sparked off specifically by Brecht's dislike of Hanns Johst's sentimentally larded play, *The Lonely One*) celebrated the life of the body and the incorrigible sameness of physical existence. At a time when other writers were rediscovering Schopenhauer, *Baal*, in emulation of Frank Wedekind's *Earth Spirit* (*Erdgeist*), asserted the vitalist values of Friedrich Nietzsche.

Yet, although *Baal* was directed against the Utopian designs of the later Expressionists, the play retained certain distinctively Expressionist features. Just like other Expressionist heroes, Baal has his moments of 'ecstasy':

> BAAL (*rising ecstatically, full of sun*): My soul is the sunlight that remains in the diamond buried in the deepest rock. And the urge of the trees, still in the grip of winter's frost, to blossom in spring. And the moaning of the cornfields as they roll under the wind. And the sparkle in the eyes of two insects who want to eat one another[4]

In conceiving Baal as a larger-than-life, mythical figure, Brecht was making full use of the Expressionist writer's licence to overstep the limits of psychological probability. What unites the play is not a traditional plot, nor the empirical sequence of a biography, but an Expressionist vision of life's *essence* as a struggle between the forces of vitality and decay. The 'open', episodic structure of this type of drama was later to become one of the defining features of Brecht's Epic Theatre. Brecht's ambition to restore to drama the function of giving shape to the major issues and 'geistige Kämpfe' (intellectual struggles) of the times – including a vision of man's future development – was a further inheritance of the Expressionist rebellion against the detailed milieu studies of the Naturalists, and one that was to issue in his later claim to have brought about a 'Copernican revolution' in the theatre. His free, poetic use of the stage as a mirror of the protagonist's inner world was also indebted to the Expressionist break with naturalistic theatrical methods, without which his own later, constructed stage designs, although very different in style, might well not have evolved. The rapid succession of short scenes in *Baal* demands a bare, flexible stage layout, which was achieved at its premiere in Leipzig (1923) by the use of a curved backcloth or cyclorama (*Rundhorizont*); some 35 years later Mother Courage's wagon was shown before just such a backdrop. The Expressionists' view of the stage as a spiritual or intellectual space, despite Brecht's rebellion against what most of them had to say, provided a model from which he could develop his own conception of a 'theatre for the scientific age'. *Baal* was one of the stages by which he made that progression.

With the outbreak of the 'German Revolution' in November 1918 it seemed possible that various hopes for a radical change in German society might be realized. Some of the Expressionist idealists (Landauer, Toller, Mühsam) even found themselves at the centre of revolutionary political activity when a short-lived 'soviet republic' came into being in Bavaria. In the event, however, the German Revolution achieved neither the dictatorship of the proletariat which was the aim of the Communists, nor the spiritual renewal which was the goal of the Utopian Expressionists, but rather the abdication of the Emperor and the creation of a parliamentary democracy. Nevertheless, Expressionist dramas dealing with revolt and revolution enjoyed their theatrical hey-day in the first years of the new Republic. By 1922, however, both public and critics had grown decidedly tired of plays elaborating the abstract dialectics of revolution and making appeals to the essential goodness of Man. The visionary pathos of this type of Expressionism had come to appear increasingly irrelevant to the day-to-day problems of sheer survival in a country beset by rampant inflation, unemployment and blackmarketeering. The immediate and considerable success, in 1922, of Brecht's second play, *Drums in the Night*, which ends with the hero taking his cynical farewell of the revolution, reflected this change in the public's mood. Herbert Jhering, at that time a rising young theatre critic who was to champion Brecht's cause throughout the Twenties, claimed, after seeing the first performance of this play, 'Brecht has changed the literary complexion of Germany overnight.'[5]

Drums in the Night tells the story of Andreas Kragler, a German infantryman who returns to Berlin in November 1918 after spending most of the war in a prisoner of war camp in Africa, only to discover that his girlfriend, Anna, believing him to be dead, has become engaged to, and is pregnant by, another man. Kragler's usurper is Friedrich Murk, who, like Herr Balicke (Anna's father), has made a fortune out of the war while 'the Kraglers' were suffering or dying in their millions. Both Murk and the Balickes

connect the returning Kragler in their minds with 'Sparta-
cus', the Communist organisation that aimed to unite the
workers and the returning soldiery, many of them still
armed, in the revolutionary transformation of Germany.
Kragler, however, has no such radical plans in mind. He is,
rather, very afraid of not being able to re-establish contact
with normal life after his war-time experiences, or to put it
in the imagery of the play, he fears having become a 'ghost'.
The discovery that Anna, because of her pregnancy,
cannot or will not have him back hits him very hard,
confirming his worst fears.

In the course of a bout of heavy drinking, Kragler lands
in a cheap pub not far from Berlin's newspaper district
where some of the severest clashes between the revolutionaries and the forces still loyal to the government took
place. Here Kragler, becoming increasingly bitter and
drunk, pours out his story to an eager audience, eventually
going off with the other drunks to join the fighting. What
motivates this decision, however, is not revolutionary zeal,
since he does not believe that the world can be changed, but
an impulse to commit suicide in the grand manner: 'Making
an end of things is better than schnapps. It's no joke. It's
better to disappear than to sleep.'[6] Before he reaches the
scene of the fighting, he is intercepted by Anna, and this
meeting makes him choose life rather than death, a 'big
white bed' shared with her rather than ending up 'like a
drowned cat on the asphalt'. The others reproach him with
treachery and cowardice, but Kragler, with feelings com-
pounded of guilt and anger, rejects their claims on him,
together with the audience's (assumed) demand that he go
off and die as any decent tragic hero would:

KRAGLER : You almost drowned in your tears for me and
I've just washed my shirt in your tears. Is my flesh to

rot in the gutter so that your idea can get into heaven? Are you drunk? (. . .) I'm a swine and the swine's going home.[7]

For a contemporary audience the antithesis between this final scene and that of, say, Ernst Toller's *The Transformation*, in which the hero Friedrich leads the masses off to create a brave new world, could not have been plainer.

Brecht's attack on Expressionism was conveyed not only through the hero's explicit rejection of the claims of an 'idea' on his loyalty, but also through the form and style of *Drums in the Night*. Instead of the abstract settings and symbolic figures of the Expressionist drama, Brecht set his play in contemporary Berlin and described the difficulties of an ordinary soldier in adjusting to what he encounters there. His play was also cast in the familiar five-act form, and had a conventional love triangle for its plot. In later years Brecht, much embarrassed by the reactionary political message of this play, was also very dismissive of its conventional organisation. As with so many of Brecht's retrospective comments on his early work, these strictures are very misleading.

In the first place, the play was no simple return to realism. As well as employing the deliberately 'crass' techniques of the satirist Carl Sternheim, the play contained obvious travesties of Expressionist style – sets painted in the Expressionistic diagonal manner, for example, and an all too obviously symbolic red moon that glowed automatically whenever Kragler appeared on stage, so as to convey visually, and funnily, the 'Expressionistic' moods of hysteria that had seized Germany in the wake of the war. Secondly, despite Brecht's denial of this fact, the play already made use of what was later to be called the 'technique of alienation': the action was interrupted, the audience was addressed directly, the theatricality of the theatre was made explicit, authorial commentary was provided in the form of placards hung in the auditorium, bearing such slogans as 'Don't gape so romantically' and 'Every man is the best in his own skin'. Thirdly, Brecht's disavowal of the sentimental and 'conventional' features of this play obscures the fact that his later work also makes use of such elements, often hinging on an appeal to simple, strong emotions – as in the *Caucasian Chalk Circle*, say, where the 'love triangle' involves two mothers in competition for a child, one of whom lays claim to the audience's sympathy just as strongly as Andreas Kragler in *Drums in the Night*. As an exercise in using the resources of drama and stage to manipulate the responses of the audience, *Drums in the Night* was an important part of Brecht's theatrical apprenticeship.

The nearest thing the Twenties had to a period style in Germany was the so-called 'New Sobriety' or 'New Objectivity' – *die neue Sachlichkeit* – a label that loosely holds together various features of a general aversion to effusion and pathos, whether of an imperialist, pro-war persuasion or of the Expressionist, anti-war variety. Andreas Kragler's homecoming illustrates this feeling that it was high time to sober up: specifically, he has to learn that he must regain control of his emotions if he is to salvage what is left in his relationship with Anna. On the level of style and form, the various distancing techniques employed in *Drums in the Night* were part of the same anti-emotional trend. On the other hand, Brecht retained an understanding of and sympathy for passion, with the result that his plays were generally informed by a tension between the need to release and the need to control passion. His next play, for example, *In the Jungle* (1923; re-titled *In the Jungle of the Cities* (*Im Dickicht der Städte*) in 1927) depicts a wild, idiosyncratic struggle for dominance between two men whose passion for conflict leads them to sacrifice virtually everything they had seemed to live for until the point when their all-consuming fight began. Though the theme of the play is the emotional savagery still underlying the surface of the modern city-dweller's life, it is presented in an opaque, densely metaphorical style that acts as a filter for the characters' emotions, with many half-parodistic quotations of popular forms of entertainment (gangster films and Westerns, boxing and wrestling matches), and with a 'cold, unreal Chicago' for its setting.

A similar, but theatrically more effective combination of passion and control resulted from Brecht's next experiment, his adaptation and production at the Munich Kammerspiele (chamber theatre) in 1924 of Marlowe's *The Life of Edward the Second*. There was much discussion at the time as to how – or whether – the classical repertoire should be performed after a war which had produced such profound changes in European life that the relevance to the present of past culture was open to question. Brecht's answer was characteristically radical: he advocated and practised an attitude of 'healthy vandalism' towards the works of the past, freely plundering them for their *Materialwert* ('value as raw material'), and claiming the right to impose on them whatever point of view seemed appropriate to the needs of the present.[8] (This was also, broadly speaking, how he approached the many adaptations he made after the Second World War, from a Marxist standpoint, though by that time he had learned to temper his impertinence towards the classics who were possibly even more revered in Socialist than in bourgeois circles, and to speak rather of clarifying and emphasizing the socially critical substance of the original).[9]

The young Brecht's critical champion, Herbert Jhering,

claimed that Brecht's adaptation of *Edward II* (*Leben Eduards des Zweiten von England*) (the first production for which he carried full personal responsibility) was a 'historic achievement' because of Brecht's substitution of 'distance' for 'grandeur' (*Größe*) in his view of the classical hero: 'He did not make these people small. He did not atomise the figures. He set them at a distance. He took away from the actor the right to importune the audience with the soulfulness (*Gemütlickeit*) of his temperament. He insisted that they give an account of the *events* of the play. He demanded simple gestures from them. He forced them to speak coolly and clearly. No emotive cheating was tolerated. This produced the objective, "epic" style.'[10]

The methods of direction and staging that produced this effect anticipate Brecht's later work with the Berliner Ensemble. The tiny stage of the Kammerspiele did not pretend to be anything other than a stage. In fact the set (designed by Caspar Neher) signalled its own theatricality by imitating the characteristics of a travelling show at the fairs the young Brecht was fond of frequenting. It showed a 'rapidly assembled fairground theatre. The materials used: wood, paper, coarse cloth. The sack-like costumes of the actors are daubed with the same green mortar as the walls of London'.[11] This set brought out the affinity of Brecht's text with the *Moritat* or lurid popular ballad, an effect reinforced by bringing on to the streets of London a ballad-monger complete with placards and hurdy-gurdy (a symbol of life's monotony and exiguousness that is also heard in *Baal* and *The Threepenny Opera*). By working in this convention of 'primitive' theatre Brecht was able to use simple, direct, or to use his term, 'naive' means of narration: when the soldiers were afraid he had their faces painted white (following the suggestion of the popular farceur, Karl Valentin); a single rope bound round the hands of the rebellious peers was enough to change them into prisoners.

Such simplicity did not preclude precision, but the combination of both took much rehearsal time to achieve. The actors, accustomed to thinking of the stage as a place to 'emote', were taken aback when Brecht made them repeat 'mechanical' operations – such as the roping-together of the peers, or the preparations made for Gaveston's execution – again and again, until they could perform them smoothly and convincingly. Brecht described the effect thus: 'The hanging of Gaveston was carried out very precisely, it was a special 'turn' (*Nummer*) in itself. One could become melancholy over the sad fate of Gaveston, and at the same time take pleasure in the skill with which he is hanged on the branch'[12] – and presumably also be entertained by the song Brecht had the executioner sing as he stood on a ladder above Gaveston. The 'palace of varieties' quality of the performance was enhanced by the way Brecht had the stage and properties constructed so as to make the actors show their agility and dexterity (what Brecht later described as *Artistik*), requiring them to run along narrow plank-ways or wield oversized weapons: 'Properties were made according to theatrical principles. The wooden axes, broadswords and pikes of the soldiers forced the actor into making a particular acrobatic movement.'[13]

It would be wrong to conclude from all this, however, that the performance lacked realism or emotive effect. Within the framework of acknowledged artifice Brecht expected the actors to speak and gesture in a way that they themselves felt to be naturalistic, only occasionally asking for an 'exaggerated form of Expressionism' in certain of Edward's long tirades.[14] Possibly because of the intimate scale of the Kammerspiele stage, Brecht's general preference was for small, understated gestures, which, precisely because they left things unsaid, were suggestive in effect. Brecht mostly cultivated an indirect approach to emotional matters, often balancing elements of pathos and bathos (as in the hanging of Gaveston) against one another, but this avoidance of Expressionist over-statement had the effect of making the horror of events *more* rather than less palpable (as the same technique still does in the 'comedies' of Friedrich Dürrenmatt).

Though Brecht insisted that most of the actors play in a 'thin and mean' manner, what he gave them to perform was a violent story, the dramatic impact of which he had deliberately intensified in his reworking of a number of Marlowe's scenes. The oversized swords did not simply function as vaulting poles, they also 'sparkled in the light and produced a gruesome clang'.[15] The sensuous aspect of staging was carefully exploited, the graininess of the simple, rough materials, the clang and glitter of the swords, the rattle of the steel net hanging across the stage (signifying a dungeon) whenever Edward backed into it, forcing him to spring away and spin round in horror. The sense of pent-up menace amongst the people of London was conveyed by their hasty, whispered, litany-like intonation of the refrain of the ballad-monger's satirical song 'Prayfor-us, prayforus' in a way that one spectator (the writer, Marieluise Fleißer) 'felt on her nerve-ends'. Both Erwin Faber (who played Edward) and Maria Koppenhöfer (who played his spurned wife, Anna) were allowed to play in a fully emotional style that was made all the more striking by the general manner of indirectness and understatement around them. Although irritated by the excessive length of the performance (due to a number of unfortunate accidents, such as the drunkenness of the actor – Oskar Homolka – playing Mortimer), this is how the journalist

Roda Roda summed up his experience of the premiere: 'If there be any justice *in literis et artibus*, this work should tour the whole world. From the first scene to the last it is loaded with temperament and tension, the plot devastating, the language overwhelming, the technique perfect. But: it needs to be cut. (. . .) Brecht has emerged as a powerful commander of the stage.'[16]

A Man's a Man (*Mann ist Mann*) (or *Man equals Man*, as the title has also been translated) was Brecht's first attempt at a full-length dramatic parable, a genre in which he cast many of his later, Marxist works. At this point, however, Brecht was not yet a Marxist. The lesson taught by this parable is summed up in an interlude address spoken by the Widow Begbick:

> Mr Bertolt Brecht maintains man equals man
> – A view that has been around since time began.
> But Mr Bertolt Brecht also points out how far one can
> Manoeuvre and manipulate that man.
> Tonight you are going to see a man reassembled like a car
> Leaving all his individual components just as they are.
>
> (2i, 38)

At the centre of the play stands Galy Gay, a 'donkey who is willing to carry on living as a swine' (2i, 111). As in Brecht's previous plays, life is shown in *A Man's a Man* to be an undignified struggle of all against all. But in this play Brecht's interest lies principally with a figure who is the antithesis of those earlier protagonists whose ambition was to assert their individual wills and to test their personal qualities to the very limit by seeking out opportunities for conflict. Galy Gay is a passive hero who is dragged involuntarily into life's struggles and has his identity transformed, virtually overnight, from that of a peaceable

31

harbour porter into that of 'Jeriah Jip, the human fighting machine'. Here the role of the stubborn individualist is taken by 'Sergeant Fairchild, known as Bloody Five', who represents a fierce parody of the values held by, say, Edward II, for he is prepared to castrate himself with an army revolver rather than lose his name as an embodiment of soldierly virtue. Galy Gay's wisdom and strength, by contrast, lie in his adaptability, and in his certain conviction that nothing is more important in life than satisfying his physical appetites.

The parable is cast in the style of a Chaplinesque farce, with Galy Gay as the sympathetic underdog who eventually turns the tables on his persecutors. Both the parabolic and the farcical aspects of the play are bound up with Brecht's desire to master life, the one by making it yield a definable thesis or moral, the other by setting life forcibly at a distance, translating it into the artificial language of comedy. Yet the precariousness of such mastery is equally apparent. Even when reduced to a formula, the instability of human existence remains a painful fact. And there is a price to be paid for Galy Gay's survival by non-resistance, that of being reduced to the status of a clown, a *Gummimensch* (rubber man), pushed around and moulded into whatever shape life's next contingency dictates. While farce permits the spectator the illusion of standing at a sovereign distance from the ridiculous squabbles of the characters, the laughter it provokes is no less an act of violence than those perpetrated by the fictional figures. Brecht's parables derive their theatrical life from such tensions between the intellectual and irrational elements in their composition, between their claim to have got a firm grip on life and the fact that they are so evidently still in its grip.

Despite the change of style and genre, then, *A Man's a*

Man was informed by the same mixed attitude to violence
as pervaded Brecht's earlier plays. The same is true of the
two operas he wrote (or completed) in 1928 and 1929, *The
Threepenny Opera* and *Rise and Fall of the City of
Mahagonny* (both of them parables), the last full-scale
works he wrote before he finally committed his writing to
the propagation of Communist revolution. *The Threepenny
Opera*, an adaptation of John Gay's *The Beggar's Opera*,
shares with the original a thoroughly ambivalent view of
the roguery that it portrays. The action, set in the London
underworld at some uncertain date (a queen is on the
throne, but lorries are on the streets), centres on the
conflict between Jonathan Jeremiah Peachum, proprietor
of a firm of fraudulent beggars, and Macheath, leader of a
gang of robbers, who precipitates the clash by secretly
marrying Peachum's daughter, Polly. In other words, the
plot is another variant on the theme of personal contest
between two males already used in *Baal* (Baal–Ekart),
Drums in the Night (Kragler–Murk), *In the Jungle* (Sohlink–
Garga) and *Edward II* (Mortimer–Edward). Peachum and
Macheath are contrasting types, the scheming rationalist
and the man of impulse or instinct, the repressive father-
figure and the self-indulgent, erotically successful younger
man. (Macheath was originally described by Brecht as 'the
young gentleman, adored by the ladies', one of numerous
features of his first, successful version that he subsequently
obscured.)

The action of *The Threepenny Opera*, as in Gay's original,
was also intended to be understood satirically, the avarice
and treachery of those who inhabit the underworld representing by metonymy the lack of human decency on all
levels of society: low life as a mirror of high life. However,
Brecht's satire is not yet of the kind he practised as a
Marxist, for it locates the causes of man's inhumanity to

man both in man's own nature and in that of the world at large, rather than in specific socio-economic arrangements. The world is acknowledged to be cold and dark, but those who live in it do not believe it could ever be otherwise:

> PEACHUM : Let's practise goodness: who would disagree?
> But sadly on this planet while we're waiting
> The means are meagre and the morals low.
> To get one's record straight would be elating
> But our condition's such it can't be so.
>
> (2,ii, 33)

Fierce though the conditions of their life are, the beggars, crooks and whores of *The Threepenny Opera* are far from cast down by this fact. Rather, they practise a cheerful form of cynicism as they go about the nasty, but nonetheless highly enjoyable business of doing one another down. The style of the opera, too, with its mix of picaresque farce and melodrama, is equally bent on getting as much fun as it can out of the world as it is. Although dashed off quickly to earn some money, *The Threepenny Opera* was the most popular work Brecht wrote in the Twenties (it still remains very popular today – particularly in the GDR), much more so than the experimental works in which he had invested greater effort and thought. Once he became a Marxist, particularly at first, his experimental plays once again tended to lose touch with the things that keep an audience in their seats. The achievement of the plays of the later Thirties and Forties was to recover the endangered sense of fun and vitality of his early work and harness it to his ideological aims.

3
Theories of Theatre

Reflections on the theatre accompanied Brecht's creative writing throughout his career. Even before he became known to the wider public as a playwright Brecht had begun to develop the reputation of an *enfant terrible* through the column he wrote as theatre critic for the organ of the Independent Socialist Party in Augsburg (the *Augsburger Volkswille*) in which he brought higher artistic and intellectual demands to bear on the productions of the local repertory theatre than its management, directors and actors were apparently capable of meeting. From the mid-1920s his pronouncements on drama and theatre began to take on a sociological character, and the end of that decade saw the first of his attempts to establish systematic links between Marxist ideology and Epic Theatre, links which gave rise to such terms as the 'theatre of the scientific age' or 'dialectical theatre'. Consequently, it is not possible to discuss 'Brecht's theory of theatre' as if it were a unified body of thought, for not only did his views on theatre change with his adoption of Marxism, but his definitions of the nature and function of theatre after that point varied considerably over the years, from the severely utilitarian position taken in the 'Notes on the opera *Mahagonny*' (1930) to his retraction, in the 'Short Organum for the Theatre' (*Kleines Organon für das Theater*) (1948), of his earlier decision to 'emigrate from the realm of the merely enjoyable' (BT, 180). On the other hand there was also greater continuity in his practice – and hence also in his underlying conception – of theatre than the shifts of theoretical position might suggest. Clearly, this is a topic which needs to be dealt with by stages.

Brecht's early observations on theatre express a mass of competing, even contradictory values, which, as far as he was concerned, was only right and natural: 'A man with one theory is lost. He needs several of them, four, lots! He should be able to stuff them in his pockets like newspapers, hot from the press always, you can live well surrounded by them, there are comfortable lodgings to be found between the theories.' (D, 42) In his reviews for the *Augsburger Volkswille*, for example, he was for ever demanding that the productions should have 'intellectual format' or an 'intellectual vision', while yet being very ready to respond to the emotional values of performance, praising any actor who 'shaped his role from within' with such epithets as 'powerful', 'moving', 'genuine', 'deeply affecting', and dismissing acting that he considered 'hollow' or to be 'purely external' (GW 15, 3–39 passim). He was as capable of showing his excitement at a powerful performance of Franz Moor in Schiller's *The Robbers* ('the vitality of this figure, the intellectual impetus, the physical humanity of it – this takes one's breath away' – GW 15, 22), as he was of sending up the plot of this play or *Cabal and Love* (*Kabale und Liebe*) (also by Schiller) in a brief but devastating parody.

The kind of theatre that most excited Brecht was one that satisfied *simultaneously* his sensuous, emotional and intellectual demands (or appetites, as he was fond of calling them). On the other hand, this ideal of synthesis or balance is frequently lost sight of as he responds to opposing pulls at different times. Thus, in 1920 he describes his attitude in the theatre as that of a 'beast of prey': 'I have to destroy something, I'm not used to eating plants. That's why it often smells of fresh meat in the grass, and the souls of my heroes were very colourful landscapes with clear contours and strong air. The stamping of combatants calms me, those who tear each other apart emit imprecations that satisfy me, and the little, angry screams of the damned give me ease' (GW 15, 46–7). All this has evident relevance to *Baal* or *In the Jungle*, about which, however, he also wrote the following in 1922: 'There is one common artistic error which I hope I've avoided in *Baal* and *Jungle*, that of trying to carry people away. Instinctively I've kept my distance and ensured that my effects (both of a poetic and a philosophical kind) are kept within the confines of the stage.' (D, 159)[1]

That Brecht had not simply changed his mind in the two years between these contrasting observations is evident from his later 'Address to the Gentleman in the Stalls' (1925), in which he analyses the attraction which *In the Jungle* holds for the contemporary spectator: 'I knew that you want to sit down there calmly, and pass judgement on the world, while at the same time putting your understanding of human nature to the test by placing bets on the one or other of the characters (. . .) You consider it valuable to participate in certain *meaningless* feelings of enthusiasm and discouragement, which are part of the fun of living. Taking all this together, I have to make it my aim to strengthen your appetite in my theatre. Were I to be so successful that you felt like smoking a cigar, and were I then to outdo myself by ensuring that your cigar goes out at particular points determined in advance by me, both you and I will be satisfied with me – which always remains the most important thing of all' (GW 15, 75).

At the heart of Brecht's early remarks on theatre was the conviction that theatre ought, by sensuous means, to convince the spectator of the *vitality* of the play's characters, whose individuality 'should be what we gain from the plays.' (GW 15, 50). If this led him on occasion to deprecate 'the grand drama of ideas' as practised by Friedrich Hebbel (a nineteenth-century tragedian who took a view of history similar to Hegel's), it did not prevent him, on the other hand, from envisaging, 'a divine farce in the style of El Greco, concerned with events of an ideal nature, in a drama of ideas filled with corporeality and malice' (GW 15, 55). Although strongly attracted to the idea of a naive, childlike theatre of fun (*Spaß*) which would have the same kind of appeal to the ordinary spectator as sport or the circus, Brecht also understood what Nietzsche called the 'pathos of distance', that 'motionless and ice cold air that surrounds the highest intellectual exercises – where right and duty fade away and the individual becomes isolated, filling the world, and relationships prove to be neither necessary nor possible' (D, 19).

Just as he was in search of a theatre combining emotion with control, the young Brecht wanted to achieve a synthesis of popularity with intellectuality, such as he claimed (not very plausibly), was achieved in the performances of Karl Valentin. Valentin was a popular Munich slapstick comedian with the appearance of a stick insect and a gift for entangling himself in hopeless muddles which, to Brecht's intellectual eye, signified 'the inadequacy of all things, including ourselves'. (GW 15, 39) Brecht further

38

ascribed to Valentin the ability to impart such wisdom to his beer-hall audiences subliminally, through the physical qualities of his clowning: 'When this man, one of the most memorable intellectual figures of our times, demonstrates physically to simple people the connections between imperturbability, stupidity and enjoyment of life, the cart-horses laugh and note the lesson deep within themselves' (ibid). Whatever the dramatist's aim, whether to address his work to the intellectual *Spieltrieb* (instinct for play) of a sophisticated audience, or to teach useful, practical lessons to ordinary people, the theatre could only be effective, in the opinion of the young Brecht, if the physicality of the medium was directed at the instincts of the spectator.

In the early Twenties, in the train of his aversion to the preachiness of Expressionism, Brecht even went so far as to claim that the dramatist whose aim was to teach or influence his public had actually to hide his ideas, smuggling them into his plays along with full-blooded characters so that the ideas would be 'incorporated into the instincts of the spectator, flooding through his veins like blood in a transfusion' (GW 15, 43). By the mid-1920s Brecht had lost his initial hostility to the *direct* expression of ideas in the drama, and by the end of the 1920s he had moved to the opposite pole of insisting that the modern dramatist should address his work primarily to the spectator's reason *rather* than to his feelings. Although Brecht later modified this position by allowing that a range of rather virtuous emotions, such as the scientist's excitement about a new discovery, or anger at injustice, could be properly invoked in the theatre, his mature theory continued to insist that the appeal to reason, even if made in a pleasurable manner, was the central aim of Epic Theatre. Examination of his theatrical practice, however, indicates that, far from having forgotten his early convictions about the importance of the theatre's sensuous, emotive – and largely subliminal – appeal to the instincts of the audience, his Marxist works continued to attempt (though not always successfully) to harness such effects to the rhetorical pursuit of his ideological aims.

Once Brecht had adopted Marxism he sought to develop a theory of theatre based on what he took to be central Marxist and Leninist tenets. The fact that his views attracted criticism from the proponents of a quite different aesthetic, one that also claimed to be based on Marxism and which for a long time enjoyed the approval of the guardians of Marxist–Leninist orthodoxy in Moscow, indicates that the connections Brecht asserted between his vision of theatre and Marxist–Leninist theory were contentious, but this is not a controversy that need detain us here.[2] Brecht's chief argument for theatrical innovation was that history demanded it: 'The old form of drama does not make it possible to represent the world as we see it today'. (GW 15, 173) By this he meant both that the world had changed or was in the process of changing objectively, and that man's view of his world had changed from that of earlier generations.

The objective change Brecht had in mind was the historical transition from the bourgeois age to that of the working class, from the organisation of society on the economic basis of capitalism to its organization on the basis of a socialist economy. The 'old' form of theatre, which now needed to be abolished, had been part of the ideological superstructure of capitalist society. Because the bourgeois age was one founded on individual enterprise, the drama of that age had focused attention on the individual, particularly on the great or problematic individual, in such a way as to invite the audience to empathise or identify with the experiences of the protagonist whose function was to exemplify the complexity of timeless human nature. This type of drama, although still practised, had become antiquated, so Brecht argued, because the individual had ceased to be a factor of major social and economic importance. Within the capitalist system itself the historical-materialist dialectic had led to the era of the individual entrepreneur being superseded by the emergence of vast, complex, impersonal organisations, the development and operation of which was largely unaffected by the personality of the individual who was the founder or nominal head of the firm. As Brecht put it in a characteristically provocative way, 'the Ford factory, considered technically, is a Bolshevist organisation'. (GW 15, 152) The 'old' form of drama was now useless, not only because the individual was no longer at the centre of the historical stage, but also because the impersonal and collective forces shaping the modern world did not offer, as the individual had once done, a focus for the empathetic understanding on which Aristotelian theatre had relied.

The subjective historical change that demanded the creation of a new form of theatre was the progress of the age of science. By this Brecht understood both the growing importance of the natural sciences for man's understanding and exploitation of the material world, and the relatively recent application of scientific methods to the study of human behaviour and the history of society. The classic examples of this science of society were, in Brecht's view, to be found in the writings of Marx, Engels and Lenin. With the spread of the scientific outlook throughout society the modern theatre must expect that the audience will bring to bear on its representations of life the cool, investigative eye of the scientist. Where such an attitude was not yet developed in the spectator, the task of the theatre was to stimulate it.

To meet the requirements of a theatre for the scientific age, both the subject matter of drama and its techniques of presentation had to change. Human behaviour, for example, was to be studied 'as a variable of the milieu', on the Marxist assumption that '*das gesellschaftliche Sein bestimmt das Denken*' ('social existence determines thought'). Instead of focusing (as he alleged was the case in Aristotelian theatre) on the supposedly timeless qualities and problems of human nature, as if this were simply a given of existence, like the saltiness of the sea, the dramatist should direct attention to the historically changeable features of behaviour that promote and are promoted by particular forms of social organisation. This concentration on the social processes determining people's lives was intended to reflect the 'objective' historical change mentioned above (the decreased importance of the individual), while at the same time encouraging a relativist, practical, problem-solving view of the difficulties created in people's lives by deficiencies in their societies. The traditionally pre-eminent genre of tragedy, with its emphasis on the ineluctable, fated character of human suffering and its effect of arousing the feelings of terror and pity in the audience, would have no place in the theatre of the scientific age. For Brecht this was not a matter of denying the existence of suffering, but of asserting that the most productive function for drama was to direct attention to the socio-historical, and hence remediable causes of suffering.

In order to enable the audience to view critically the patterns of cause and effect in the drama, the dramatist had to devise means of inhibiting any tendency the spectator might have to understand and evaluate the world from the

point of view of the principal *dramatis personae*. Largely
ignoring the fact that the 'old' drama relied as much on
irony for its effects as it did on identification with the
protagonist, Brecht contrasted the Aristotelian concept of
empathy unfavourably with his own concept of *Verfremdung*, which can be variously translated as estrangement,
alienation or de-familiarisation. The term refers to two
related effects: the inhibition of emotional identification,
and the opening of a fresh perspective on aspects of life that
tend to be protected from critical examination by our
over-familiarity with them. Brecht defined the learning
process produced by *Verfremdung* as a dialectical, 'triadic'
progression, moving from 'understanding' (in a false,
habitual manner), through 'non-understanding' (because
of the de-familiarising presentation), and back to 'understanding' (in a new way). To achieve this effect he
prescribed that a range of special techniques be employed
in the areas of dramatic construction and language, acting
and staging, a number of which will be discussed in the
following chapter on his practice of theatre.

The most widely used designation for Brecht's theatre,
and one which remains useful despite his later doubts about
it, is 'Epic Theatre'. Like *Verfremdung*, Brecht's conception of the 'epic' was an amalgam of different ideas.
Initially, it carried the connotation of heroic poetry, and,
although this aspect of the term is not given much
prominence in his Marxist theory, it continued to affect his
practice after 1930 – as in his dramatisation of Gorki's *The
Mother*, where ordinary people are presented with simplicity, 'as one reports the words and deeds of the great'
(GW 17, 1053). 'Epic' was further connected in Brecht's
mind with a detached, dispassionate manner of presentation ('epic calm'), and in this sense was contrasted with the
dramatic or emotive type of theatre that he considered

unscientific. The most important meaning of the term, however, was 'narrative'. Epic theatre was defined by the introduction (or re-introduction) into the theatre of a narrator or narrative voice whose function was to intervene between the events imitated in the action and the audience. The need for this epic narrator arose from the objective and subjective historical changes to which the theatre of the scientific age responded. The narrator could bring to bear on the action the scientific awareness which the characters might well lack, but which was necessary for the audience to reach an informed judgement of the events depicted. The narrator could also supply background information about complicated socio-historical processes reaching far beyond the immediate experience of individuals, and hold together in a unity of argument a variety of events or strands of action which did not constitute a 'unity of action' in the sense prescribed by Aristotelian theory.

The most straightforward description of the narrative character of epic theatre is to be found in Brecht's essay of 1938 entitled 'The Street Scene. A Basic Model for an Epic Theatre' (*Die Straßenszene. Ein Grundmodell für ein Episches Theater*) (BT, 121–9). The practical purpose of theatre is exemplified by the situation of an eyewitness to an accident who describes the sequence of events leading up to it, illustrating the behaviour of those involved by 'quoting' their movements, their gestures, their manner, in as far as these seem relevant to the goal of establishing where the responsibility lay for the accident. The narrator's aim is not to *impersonate* the characters in this everyday drama but to *describe* their interaction (or '*Gestus*' as Brecht called it) with sufficient objectivity and in as much detail as is necessary to enable the 'jury' to analyse the sequence of cause and effect and to estimate the degree of responsibility to be borne by each party involved.

The scientific model of theatre was not consistently adhered to by Brecht, not in theory and even less so in practice. Whereas the (much quoted) table of antitheses included in his 'Notes to the opera *Rise and Fall of the City of Mahagonny*' (BT, 33–42) initially contained the clear opposition 'Reason-Feeling', subsequent editions contained a footnote claiming that no outright antithesis was intended, but simply a shift of emphasis. Brecht tried to deny the inconsistency by claiming that science was actually not something unemotional, in that it involved the excitement of discovery. However, the analogy is quite unconvincing, for although it is possible to be emotional *about* science, emotions have no place in the procedures of science, whereas the theatre, even as Brecht himself practised it, is intrinsically bound up with the emotions.

The same objection applies to his analogy between a forensic investigation and his 'new' theatre. On the one hand he claimed that the modern spectator does not wish to have somebody else form judgements on his behalf, while on the other hand he insisted that Epic Theatre should have no truck with 'false objectivity'. In asserting that anger about injustice was an emotion that had its rightful place in Epic Theatre, he undermined rather than underlined the connection between his theatre and any court worth its salt. Anger at injustice may surround a trial, and may even find some controlled expression in the sentence imposed on a convicted criminal, but emotions should not be allowed to enter the process of determining guilt. Brecht's theatre, on the other hand, was avowedly partisan and incontestably emotive both in its selection and its presentation of 'evidence' to the audience or 'jury'.

In contrast to his claim that theatre should be concerned to preserve the spectator's freedom of response, Brecht's practical work as a producer and writer was directed to *manipulating* the spectator's responses. This rhetorical rather than scientific approach to theatre underlies, for example, Brecht's suggestion that a list of quanta of effect (*Wirkungsquanten* – Aj, 206) should be kept for each individual scene as part of the process of preparing a production. In fact the whole apparatus of scientific terminology with which he surrounded his theatre was itself in large measure a rhetorical device to bestow special status on his proposals.

Brecht's rhetorical approach to theatre had its own, frequently overlooked, theoretical justification in a series of propositions that cut across his claims to scientific status for his theatre. These statements add up to a theory of political theatre which fits the facts of his practice rather better than his theory of a 'theatre of the scientific age' (although he would not have wanted to admit such a distinction). Brecht's teacher in Marxism was Karl Korsch, who denied that Marx' and Engels' analysis of Capitalism could claim a scientific validity untainted by the limitations of their own historical situation, and who was promptly thrown out of the Party for his independence of mind. Like Korsch, Brecht was principally interested in Marxism as a means of effecting radical political change. From 1929 onwards his work took as its starting point Marx's observation that philosophers had for too long simply interpreted the world, whereas what mattered was to change it. He also liked to cite Lenin's assertion that revolutionaries should derive their ethics and other values from the immediate 'needs of the class-struggle'.

In philosophical, as well as political terms, Brecht's position was a pragmatist's one. Every proposition about the world, he believed, should be examined in relation to the question of whose interests it served (*cui bono*?). All thinking was to be regarded, and practised, as a form of behaviour serving particular aims: 'The truth of any statement depends on its purpose'.[3] Reality was not to be regarded as something fixed, but as defined by the human mind and shaped by human action. Unfortunately, the view of the world taken by too many people was simply a set of received ideas, the 'ruling view', which needed to be recognised in its ideological function as 'the view of the rulers'. The truth of the alternative view of the world proposed by the classic authors of Marxism–Leninism was not to be refuted by appeals to the evidence of past experiences, since these experiences were of a world not yet subject to the processes of social and mental revolution. The proof of the pudding, as he frequently observed, was in the eating. His task as a writer was to help create both that pudding (a world changed by revolution) and an appetite for it. This meant the destruction of the ideologies which kept man enslaved to misery, and the creation of a new, emancipatory 'superstructure' of ideas, the truth (that is usefulness) of which would be borne out by the new social and economic forms created by the revolution. (GW 20, 10)

In the area of Brecht's artistic work his philosophical pragmatism expressed itself in his lack of dogmatism. During rehearsals at the Berliner Ensemble theoretical discussions tended to be frowned on as getting in the way of the main objective, which was to produce theatre that worked. Although Brecht kept insisting on the contrast between his conception of theatre and one that rested on empathy, he also contradicted this position both in theory and in practice. Not only did he create characters who would produce in the spectator varying degrees of identification, particularly where he thought an agitatory effect could be produced in this way, as in *Saint Joan of the Stockyards*, *Señora Carrar's Rifles*, *The Visions of Simone*

Machard (*Die Gesichte der Simone Machard*); he also acknowledged that the spectator of Epic Theatre identified, if not with the character being portrayed, then with the (critical) standpoint of the actor (GW 16, 622). Whereas he argued around 1930 for an ascetic conception of a theatre devoted to pedagogy and the dissemination of information, his 'Short Organum for the Theatre' (1948) argued that even revolutionary theatre should be *dulce* as well as *utile*. Whereas he subscribed on a number of occasions to the theoretical view that the notion of individual character had disintegrated, he both created rounded individuals (such as Mother Courage who would defy anyone to 'put a stamp' on her face) and repeatedly reflected, with evident satisfaction, on the growing line of new figures he had brought to life on the stage. To appreciate the pervasiveness of Brecht's pragmatism, however, we need to consider his practice at some length.

4
Brecht's Practice of Theatre

Brecht's theory was a mixture of description, prescription, polemic, and an attempt to bring his ideas on theatre into systematic relationship with Marxism. As such, it represents only an approximation to the way he actually practised theatre. This chapter will therefore describe in general terms the principal means by which he effected his ideas and certain aspects of his practice not fully provided for in his theory.

Neither Epic Theatre nor the alienation effect was simply an aspect of staging or performance. Epic and alienating features were already incorporated by Brecht into the texts of his plays before these were tried out, and in all likelihood revised repeatedly, in the theatre.

In Epic Theatre the narrative voice that interposes itself between the audience and the events enacted on stage takes on so many forms at the level both of the large- and small-scale organisation of the plays, that Brecht could quite properly claim that the 'general gesture of showing accompanies each of the particular gestures shown'

(GW 16, 697). It is evident, for example, in the types of play Brecht habitually chose. Although still relatively free of the direct narrational devices found in his later work, the productions of *Drums in the Night* and *Baal* at the beginning of the 1920s prompted reviewers to describe them as 'scenic ballads' or 'ballad-like', while his adaptation of Marlowe's *Life of Edward II* was felt to be descended from a particular kind of ballad, the lurid *Moritat*, often sung at the fairgrounds which the young Brecht was fond of frequenting, by a balladeer who pointed with a stick at a series of tableaux illustrating scenes from the versified, often moralising, story he was reciting. The looseness of the ballad form, in which episodes are held together by the voice or 'pointer' of a narrator, rather than by a plot, carried over into Brecht's historical plays. Without the inherent dynamic of an unfolding action and counter-action to carry him from scene to scene, the spectator watching *Mother Courage*, say, has to tune into the consciousness of the implicit narrator (whose presence becomes explicit in the captions introducing each scene) in order to grasp the unity of the events being enacted; in the case of *Mother Courage* this unity is constituted by an argument about the nature of war and the role played in it by ordinary people.

By placing the onus on the spectator to re-construct by inference the viewpoint of the narrator, this method of construction has the strongly suggestive effect of drawing the spectator into the perspective of the narrator. The effect is not fundamentally dissimilar to that of empathetic identification with the *dramatis personae*, to which the epic method supposedly offered an alternative. Brecht's Epic Theatre thus does not so much dispense with empathy as shift the point of identification away from the characters and onto the narrator. Yet if this is how Epic Theatre works in practice, Brecht's endlessly repeated theoretical claim that the theatre for a scientific age permits the audience to develop a detached, freely critical view of the performance, is quite misleading. In truth, Brecht's theatre is rhetorical. It is at least as persuasive in its intentions as it is analytic, and the many forms assumed by the 'epic' narrator play a crucial rhetorical role in eliciting the spectator's assent to the construction put on reality by the narrator.

Even more than the history play, Brecht favoured the theatrical parable, again a type of play where events are mediated to the audience by a narrator who invites them to reflect on what they see as an allegory (*Gleichnis*) of something specific (such as fascist racism in *Roundheads and Pointed Heads* or the rise of Hitler in *The Resistible Rise of Arturo Ui*) or as an illustration of some general theme (*A Man's a Man*, *The Good Person of Szechwan*). Even when working in a genre other than parable, such as the history play or the *Volksstück* (popular farce – *Mr Puntila and his Man Matti*) or in his adaptation of what was originally a realistic comedy, Lenz's *The Private Tutor* (*Der Hofmeister*), the presence of the didactic narrative voice introduces a parabolic quality into the writing. In his parables the narrator is often represented on stage by someone who speaks a prologue or epilogue setting out the theme of the parable (for example, 'the ABC of German misery' in *The Private Tutor*), or pointing out the moral ('the womb is still fertile from which that crawled', in *Arturo Ui*) or seemingly to demand that the audience discover their own moral (*The Good Person*). In an interlude address (*Zwischenspruch*) in *A Man's a Man* the actress playing Widow Begbick interprets the parable on behalf of the author: 'But then Herr Brecht points out how far one can / Maneouvre and manipulate that man' (2i, 38). In the *Caucasian Chalk Circle* the narrator is represented by a singer who not only links, comments on and interprets events, but acts like a director, telling the Governor to stop and look behind him, or urging Grusha to flee with the child. This is just a particularly clear example of the power attaching to the narrative voice in Epic Theatre, a power most frequently evinced by his adopting the apodictic tone of a sage who combines old and new wisdom, a firm understanding of the past with a clear view of the future, as in the ringing lines that mark the end of the *Chalk Circle*:

> That what there is shall belong to those who are good for
>   it, thus
> The children to the maternal, that they thrive;
> The carriages to good drivers, that they are driven well;
> And the valley to the waterers, that it shall bear fruit.
>
> (7, 237)

The confidently 'sovereign' stance of such a narrator offers an attractive, even seductive, object of identification in a world full of uncertainty.

The narrative voice in Epic Theatre has, then, a controlling function. It seeks to keep the dramatic characters in their place, namely subordinate to the teaching and learning process in which author and audience are assumed to be engaged. Brecht, a passionate chess-player, sometimes (but, fortunately, not always) treated his dramatic figures like pieces in a chess game, presenting them as social types or functions rather than as individuals. The narrator's control may take the form of the characters speaking in a bald manner that sounds like a first-person transformation of a third-person description, as when the teacher introduces himself in *He who said Yes*: 'I am the teacher. I have a school in the town and have a pupil whose father is dead. He now only has his mother, who looks after him. Now I am going to see them and say

52

farewell, for I am shortly to embark on a journey into the mountains' (GW 2, 15).

More frequently the narrator's presence and power are conveyed by other forms of non-naturalistic speech in which the voice of the character is overlaid by the critical tone of the narrator. This occurs when there is an element of quotation, often parodistic, in the speech of the character, as when the words of gangsters or meat-packers are cast in blank verse, or when structural and verbal allusion to scenes from *Faust I* or *Richard II* are built into Arturo Ui's meetings with Ignatius Dullfeet and his wife Betty, which in turn allude simultaneously to the career of Al Capone and to Hitler's annexation of Austria. Brecht's dialogue is full of such quotations, the defining or 'alienating' effect of which he wanted the actor to reinforce by making it clear that he in turn was quoting the words and actions of the character.

One of the most frequently encountered forms of quotation in Brecht's plays is his habit of basing characters on familiar types. Thus the figure of Joan Dark, for example, incorporates quotations not only of the heroines of Schiller's *Maid of Orleans* (*Die Jungfrau von Orleans*) and of Goethe's *Iphigenia* but also of the general literary type of the courageous but naive young idealist, while Shen Teh, whose soubriquet is 'angel of the slums', is derived from that clichéd figure of screen and novelette, the good-hearted whore. Where main characters were concerned, Brecht usually developed the figure in directions which challenged the conventional view of the type, and his theatre becomes most interesting when his sense of individual complexity led him to differentiate a character to a point where it became a genuine challenge to the typifying approach to character on which the epic narrator's control of the play's argument or demonstration depends.

Brecht's Epic Theatre has a tendency to favour certain types of action as well as character. One major type is the learning process, the most straightforward example of which is the development of Pelagea Wlassowa (in *The Mother*) from a conservative and ill-informed working-class mother into a revolutionary who can teach others about the condition of society. More often – as in *St Joan of the Stockyards* or *The Days of the Commune* (*Die Tage der Commune*) – Brecht shows an imperfect learning process, or a character who refuses to learn from experience (such as Mother Courage). This type adds to the play's demonstration of 'what is the case' in society, a warning about the consequences of not making such understanding the basis of one's actions. Another variant of the learning play is the trial, which may provide the structure of the whole play as in *The Trial of Lucullus* (*Das Verhör des Lukullus*), or emerge rapidly from the initial situation (*The Baden-Baden Cantata*, *The Decision*) or, most frequently, take place in the last scene, where it produces a summing up of the events of the plot (*The Exception and the Rule*, *The Caucasian Chalk Circle*, *The Good Person of Szechwan*). These trials as often as not produce an unacceptable verdict on the events, although they make it quite clear what the verdict should be, with the effect of adding provocation to instruction. Here again the Epic narrator shows himself to be a skilled rhetorician, who knows how to reinforce the tendency to identify with his viewpoint (as one which makes evident the errors or injustices perpetrated in the play) by offering the audience a complementary object of antipathy in the unjust judges on stage.

Narration or commentary other than by the individual dramatic characters is nothing new in the theatre. In the drama of ancient Greece, for example, these functions were performed by the Chorus, a mass of people whose fate was entangled with that of the principal characters. In Brecht's Epic Theatre, too, commentary is sometimes expressed through the medium of a chorus, as in *The Decision* where the *Kontrollchor* (examining or controlling chorus – the name is appropriate to the function of the narrator in Brecht's Epic Theatre generally) punctuates the demonstration of a group of party activists with hymns such as 'Praise of the Party' or 'Praise of Illegality'. This work, originally written for massed workers' choirs in Berlin, makes evident the collective viewpoint which the Epic Narrator in Brecht's Marxist theatre generally is assumed to represent.

Whether choral or not, the song is an important vehicle for authorial commentary. This may, like the chorus in *The Decision*, take the form of straight commentary or exhortation, whereby a character or actor simply functions as the mouthpiece of authorial views, but more often than not the commentary is implicit and ironical, as much a commentary *on* the character singing the song as one *by* him or her. In such instances the singing of the song, which is usually clearly marked off from the dramatic action by having the character come to the front of the stage to address the audience directly, provides an opportunity to underline the 'gestic' presentation of behaviour in Epic Theatre: the song isolates and focuses attention on certain important attitudes or features of behaviour – the *gestus* of resignation in the 'Song of Green Cheese' (*Szechwan*) or the contradictions in Mother Courage's commonsensical view of life in the 'Song of Capitulation'. Brecht expected the composers with whom he collaborated to help him in his task of defining the attitude of a character by producing music of an estranging character, as in, say, the refrain of the 'Cannon Song' (*The Threepenny Opera*) where the accompaniment gets ever faster, seemingly running ahead of the singers and thus giving the impression that the boastful soldiers are really far from being in command of the situation.

The Epic narrator exerts his influence most powerfully and pervasively through the language of the plays. Certain features of this – parody, allusion, quotation, third-person statements in the first-person form – have been mentioned already. There are many others. Frequently Brecht employs a witty style in order to keep the audience alert and aware that it is being engaged in an intellectual transaction. This style employs various devices to arouse and then disappoint expectations: oxymoronic formulations, as when Puntila is described as being 'sober as a newt' or as having 'attacks of total, senseless sobriety' which put him into a condition of 'diminished responsibility'; clichés which are subverted by adding a tag to them – 'Love is a divine power – I warn you'; proverbs with an element changed – 'One war doesn't make a summer'; paradox – 'dehumanised humanity, planned disorder'; metaphors which involve a clash between tenor and vehicle, as when Mother Courage, extending common parlance ('a flourishing trade'), speaks of the war as 'blossoming'. Such unexpected formulations are designed to have the ideologically unsettling effect of alienating commonly held prejudices. Apart from this functional justification, however, it is equally important to recognise the aesthetic quality or sheer entertainment value of such agile, highly polished phrasing. These extra values help to make the narratorial voice that can be heard speaking over or through the words of the dramatic figures seem attractive, and thus, at the very least, worth lending an ear to. As a good rhetorician, Brecht understood the importance of the *captatio benevolentiae*, that is, of gaining the good will of his audience.

Brecht's rhetorical bent is also evident in another aspect

of his dramatic language, one that tends not to be mentioned much because it does not fit in with the stereotype of him as the playwright of alienation. What I am referring to is his use of elevated phrasing, frequently powerfully charged with pathos to win sympathy for a view he himself endorsed. In *St Joan of the Stockyards*, for example, Brecht not only wrote pastiche and parody of classical style, but also used the freedom this non-naturalistic manner gave him to deliver ringing lines worthy of Schiller himself. Where this kind of elevated tone is used for the songs of *The Decision* and *The Mother*, Hanns Eisler's musical setting similarly aims at reinforcing rather than undercutting the emotional impact of the words. Brecht admired the elder Brueghel's arbitrary use of colour to place emphases where it suited him; Brecht's dramatic language, with its mixture of satirical, witty and pathetic effects has something of the same quality.

While working, in exile, on *The Good Person of Szechwan* Brecht complained of the impossibility of completing a play satisfactorily without access to a stage on which to try it out in practice. Although his texts were already full of invention he regarded them as only a basic sketch from which the fuller reality of theatrical performance was to be developed. Carl Weber, who worked with him at the Berliner Ensemble, recalled that he had 'never seen anyone cut a script as mercilessly as Brecht cut his own'.[1] Disconcertingly for his actors, Brecht would also rewrite sections of the text during rehearsals, sometimes introducing new script at the last minute. If a scene did not elicit the intended response from the audience when a production was opened to the public, the process of revision would be continued during the run of a play. Such prolonged experimentation with a play was, of course, only possible under the unusual conditions of operation enjoyed by the Berliner Ensemble, principally its freedom to spend up to nine months in preparation for a production which could then be kept in repertoire for a number of years.

The same experimental approach was taken not just to the text but to all aspects of production and performance. Brecht was evidently gifted with an unusual naiveté, or, as some would have it, forgetfulness, which allowed him to look at something he had written, or at some carefully produced arrangement for a scene, as if he had never seen it in his life before. For such a prolific theoretician, Brecht made very little mention of theory when developing a production, nor did he welcome theorising from others. Interested mainly in solving the problems of presentation practically and effectively (his favourite adages were 'truth is concrete' and 'the proof of the pudding is in the eating'), Brecht welcomed suggestions from his actors, provided they took the form of showing how some gesture, movement or recitation of a line could help to narrate the *Fabel* more strikingly, more entertainingly or more elegantly.

When preparing a production, Brecht's first concern was with 'blocking' the play. From early on, perhaps under the influence of silent films, he is reported as asserting that the positioning, gestures and movements of the actors should all be directed to expounding the plot so graphically that the gist of it would be clear even to a spectator unable to hear the words. Allowing for the exaggeration in this, he undoubtedly did adhere to the view that the job of the stage was, as far as possible, to give visual expression to the content of a play. Thus, when Brecht was dissatisfied with the way some scene was working 'the first thing to be reworked would be the blocking',[2] so that it would focus attention more effectively on the 'basic gestus' of the scene, that is the set of social relations, transactions and attitudes it was intended to illuminate. When he had solved such

problems to his own satisfaction he had a photographic
record or *Modellbuch* made of a production to illustrate the
basic grouping for each scene, as well as those gestures,
movements and re-groupings that marked each of the
turning-points of the action. At the beginning of *Mother
Courage*, for example, the mother and her three children
first appear as a group riding on or pulling the family
wagon. The wagon holds them in physical proximity to one
another, but also produces an arrangement of inequality:
mother and daughter are pulled while the two sons have to
do the work once done by the horse. This arrangement
introduces the themes of universal exploitation (it affects
relations even within the family unit) and of the degrada-
tion of human beings to the level of animals (an idea
constantly reinforced by the verbal imagery of the play),
and so prepares for the break-up of the family that begins
already in this opening scene when Eilif slips out of the
wagon-traces to go off with a recruiting officer. Each step
that leads to this outcome can be 'read' from the photographs that show Mother Courage trying to keep the family
grouped together and at a distance from the recruiters who
block the way, until she herself, lured behind the wagon
(which is meant to protect and provide for the family) by
one of the recruiters, lets Eilif momentarily out of her sight.

In order to allow the significance of each grouping or
change of position to emerge clearly, Brecht warned his
actors to combat a number of actorly habits: the habit of
gravitating towards the centre of the stage; of separating
from groups in order to stand alone; of drawing closer to
any person they were addressing; of looking fixedly at a
dialogue partner; of not looking at a dialogue partner at all;
of always standing side-on to the front of the stage. Scenic
arrangements had not only to bring out the significance of
any given scene, but were also made to be pleasing to the

eye, sometimes by adopting the compositional principles of historical paintings. Yet Brecht's insistence on a methodical, rationally controlled approach to grouping and movement did not preclude his use of the *suggestive* possibilities of the stage. In the scene in *The Chalk Circle*, for example, where Grusha watches over the abandoned 'high-born child', Brecht encouraged the designer, Karl von Appen, to create the effect of a crib-scene, thereby associating Grusha (another lowly handmaiden) with the figure of the Madonna. While this arrangement can be seen as adding a layer of meaning to the action by setting up a counterpoint between the stories of Mary and Jesus on the one hand and Grusha and Michael on the other, the arrangement inevitably also functions emotively, suggesting that a strong maternal bond is being formed between the girl and the child, and encouraging the formation of a related bond between the audience and the figures of mother and child.

During a fairly lengthy process of establishing the blocking for each scene Brecht would also begin to develop particular *Gesten* or details of the performance with the actors. He proceeded on the principle of 'one thing *after* another' rather than 'one thing *out of* another' in order to prevent the actors blurring or failing to develop fully the contradictions in a scene or a character. His early conviction that a 'scene in a play becomes more interesting, the more hostility there is latent within it' (GW 15, 54) was later formalised into a dialectical insistence that any given unity was always a unity of opposites, an unstable synthesis created out of contradictions. Another feature common to his early and his later work in the theatre was his demand for precision, particularly in the performance of manual operations. When directing a production of his own adaptation of Marlowe's *Life of Edward the Second* in Munich in 1924, which aimed a broadside at the 'plastercast

monumental style' of conventional Shakespearean productions, Brecht perplexed the actors by making them spend
time learning how to tie a noose properly, the sort of detail
they tended to neglect in favour of sustaining the mood or
impetus of a scene. Brecht's method, which dammed back
the *Temperament* beloved of German actors in order to
focus attention on concrete details of behaviour produced
new and complex affects that enhanced rather than diminished the dramatic force of the play. By calling attention
to the skill and even elegance with which soldiers tie a
noose before the eyes of the man who is to be hanged by it,
Brecht set up a tension between detachment and involvement that permitted the reality of the event to etch itself
into the spectator's mind more deeply than a heated – and
therefore conventional – treatment of the scene could have
achieved. As one observer remarked, Brecht's effects in
that production of *Edward II* 'sawed at the nerves'.[3] In
later productions Helene Weigel developed great mastery
of this technique of concentrating on seeming incidentals
(such as Señora Carrar's baking of bread) so as to slow
down the tempo of performance and thereby to enhance
both the element of realism and the dramatic tension.
(Carrar's dogged baking was her way of resisting the
demand that she should hand out guns needed to fight
Franco.)

To help the actor contribute to the controlled narration
of the play Brecht devised a number of rehearsal techniques that were related to his techniques of writing. These
included: translating first-person lines into the third-person
form, or the present-tense into the past; speaking the stage
directions and commentaries along with the dialogue;
substituting prose for verse; repeating a gesture while
casting the words in a variety of forms – in a lower or higher
register of speech, for example; the exchange of roles

between actors. This last device was intended to help the actors build their parts on a basis of mutual co-operation, by seeing a situation from the point of view of another character, and above all by each seeing his own role from the point of view of others. What Brecht sought to achieve thereby was a presentation of behaviour that focuses attention on social role-playing rather than on the character's innate disposition or emotional state. The actors should understand and show, for example, that the way a master behaves is conditioned by the way a servant allows him to behave – and vice versa. In this area of characterisation Brecht's repeatedly declared aversion to 'psychology' has caused considerable confusion. In practice he certainly was interested in the individuality of his characters, and of providing the audience with insights into their inner life. During rehearsals for *Galileo*, for example, he gave the following reply when asked by the actress playing Virginia (Regine Lutz), whether Galileo's daughter loved her father: 'Yes, but that is a development. He has deprived her of her real life. In the third scene she is pushed off to court, then he prevents her marriage, so that she's now a pious old maid. From the sixth scene onwards, where she's asked about her confessor, she is constantly being influenced by the Church.'[4] Such observations were clearly laying the basis for complex character-portrayal, albeit of a kind that would draw attention to the formative role of social experiences. Brecht would have made his conception of theatre clearer if, instead of polemicising generally against psychology in the theatre, he had simply insisted that in his theatre the term should always be prefaced with the word 'social'.

There would also be less confusion about Brechtian theatre if his practice had been less varied than it actually was. At times – in much of *Galileo*, for example – Brecht was creating straightforwardly realistic drama. Carl Weber, for example, wrote of his first experience of a Brechtian production that this was, 'the first time I had ever seen people on stage acting like real human beings; there was not a trace of "acting" in that performance, though the technical brilliance and perfection of every moment was stirring'.[5] Anna Seghers noted this impression of Helene Weigel's acting in the last scene of *Mother Courage*: 'She pulls her cart as Mother Courage across the barren field. Not only does she play, she *is* completely alone. The spectators are gripped by the horror of war, as if they were experiencing it for the first time.'[6] It is evident that Weigel's acting produced in Anna Seghers as much of an illusion of reality as theatre is ever capable of creating. One of the most important means whereby Weigel achieved the effect was the combination of a simple, direct, unaffected manner of delivering her lines with (where appropriate) a colouring of her native Austrian dialect. This technique was embodied by Brecht in his general advice to actors on the means that achieve a synthesis of style and naturalness. On the other hand, Brecht also worked in another, sharply caricaturing manner, partly learned from *commedia dell' arte* techniques, which required the actors to make their stylisation of speech and movement very evident. As an example of this one might take the choreography of the part of Läuffer in his adaptation of Lenz's *The Private Tutor*. When this figure first appears on stage to speak the prologue, his movements were given the quality of a mechanical doll such as one finds on a musical box. In a somewhat modified form such exaggeration of movement was carried over into the action proper, for example, in the scene where the tutor, inwardly seething, has to make a scraping bow to his employer, Major von Berg; during rehearsals, Brecht and Neher outdid one another in producing ever more extreme caricatures of this gesture. In the Ensemble production of *Arturo Ui* (made after Brecht's death) movement was enormously speeded up, both to create the effect of an early film and to give physical expression to the frenetic quality in the behaviour of the characters. Both techniques could exist side by side in a production, the one fulfilling the function of convincing the spectator that the play was presenting an image of the real world, the other asserting the epic narrator's power over the dramatic images and, usually, inviting the spectator to share with him the (sometimes violent) pleasures of taking what Brecht described as a 'sovereign' view of the world.

The mix of realism and caricature in acting methods used in Brecht's theatre was repeated in the area of staging, from costume and make-up to properties and set-design. The realism tended to be concentrated in the properties which, for historical plays, were sometimes genuine museum pieces, at other times contrived to give the impression of being so. In truth, Brecht was much less interested in naturalistic accuracy than in the expressive qualities of properties. He wanted them to exhibit the marks of human use in a way that contributed to the social statement of a scene, and he would go to endless trouble – and expense – to create by artifice the effects needed. The faded blue blouse worn by Weigel in *The Mother*, for example, was the product of long experimentation with different cloths, designs and above all with techniques of dyeing and fading, which eventually resulted in a garment that created the illusion of having been carefully washed over many years, and so reflected Brecht's conception of the way a proletarian woman would have lived in pre-Revolutionary Russia. The Berliner Ensemble followed Brecht's example in their production of his adaptation of Shakespeare's *Coriolanus*. In an interview with the *Drama Review*, the director,

Joachim Tenschert, gave this reply to a question about the seeming historical genuineness of the 'recognisably Roman' costumes and weapons used: 'Ironically, not one thing in the production is archaeologically accurate – not a costume, not a sword, not a buckle, nothing. Our work was based on very extensive research, but the research was not confined to the period in which the play takes place. Etruscan sources, for example, were very useful – statues, paintings etc. – but almost everything was stylised to make it more expressive.'[7] The shape of the short sword carried by the Roman soldiers, for example, was actually derived from a Finnish knife belonging to Weigel. The result was a very stumpy weapon, suited to stabbing rather than elegant sword play, and hence an effective means of emphasising the brutality of the action of killing.

Such things are familiar enough theatrical practices for achieving the effects of illusion and emotional impact. What makes them worthy of comment in the case of Brecht's theatre is the contrast in which they stand to his constant polemicising against illusion in other forms of theatre, and to the accompanying claim to scientific status for the images of reality presented in Epic Theatre. Brecht justified his manipulations of the appearance of things on the grounds that such artistic operations sacrificed the truth of appearances (*Augenschein*) in order to tell the truth about the *functions* of objects and people more clearly than the chance surface of reality would do by itself. In practice, however, his theatrical work was not so much a mapping of reality as a rhetorical exercise which sought to lend credibility to a set of affectively charged images of reality. His work, like that of other artists, was guided by the principle that the internal relations between the elements in any given sign-system, (such as a play) are more important for communicative purposes than the reference of individual elements to external reality, that is, because the squat swords were integrated with other elements in the play, the overall effect was to create an *illusion* of reality.

The acting technique of overt stylisation, usually to produce effects of caricature, also had its equivalent on the level of costume design. Perhaps the most obvious examples of this are the *Masken* (the German term can mean both make-up and mask) that Brecht was fond of using. His typical procedure was to exaggerate some feature of the head or face, increasing the degree of distortion in relation to a figure's identification with the prevailing class system. In *The Caucasian Chalk Circle*, for example, those of high rank were given full-face masks made of hard material, while those of lower rank, also corrupted by the system but less completely, had masks covering only part of the face and/or made of flexible material. The maid Grusha, the 'lowest of the low', with no vested interest in the system, had her status of exception to the rule of deforming alienation underlined by the fact that she wore no mask, so that her face was free, as those of the others were not, to show a wide range of human emotions. These masks were intended as alienation devices with the double function of defining the figures in terms of their social role and, by limiting the actor's reliance on facial expression, of encouraging him to use bold, demonstrative gestures. The principal effect in performance, however, is an emotional one akin to that achieved by those cartoon techniques which assign sharp or gross shapes to the 'bad' figures and idealised faces and figures to the 'goodies'. The spectator identifies with the human, vulnerable face of Grusha and reacts with a mixture of fear and dislike to the (literally) hard-faced figures who threaten her and the child. In this play, and in others, where the parabolic tendency is particularly marked, the truth about reality is presumed to be known – in broad outline at the very least – and the theatrical images have the function of creating or reinforcing associative bonds between moral, social and aesthetic – tactile values: softness, attractiveness, emotional generosity and goodness are linked with the exploited Grusha, whereas the exploiting classes and their agents are associated with hardness, ugliness and evil.

Stylisation, in other words, can work to intensify emotion rather than in the opposite direction. Here again, it is the rhetorical rather than the 'scientific' aspect of Brecht's practice that is striking. This is no less the case where, as in his direction of the actors playing the Court Scholars in *Galileo*, he added realistic details in rehearsal to modify figures who on paper seem to be strongly caricatured, or where, as in the *Chalk Circle*, he insisted that Grusha should not be too attractive or saintly. These modifications were simply the mark of a rhetorician who knew that he had to lend plausibility to his *exempla*.

Brecht liked to have his plays performed on a relatively bare stage. His favourite designer, Caspar Neher, would take as his starting point for the work on any given scene the relationships of the characters. This *gestus* he would capture in a sketch which grouped them in significant poses. The blocking and movements of the scenes were developed in conjunction with such sketches. It is reported that on occasion Brecht would not, or could not, proceed with the direction of a scene in the absence of advice from Neher about positioning. The rest of the set was then built up from a carefully selected group of properties that were functional within the action, some (usually minimal) indication of the nature of the space in which the action takes place (a door-frame or a window could represent a house, some shop-signs a street), and a backdrop which might be an empty cyclorama or a painted screen showing a free artistic evocation of, or commentary on a scene. As Eric Bentley has pointed out, this technique of staging is not adequately described if one simply says that it is a means of stressing the theatricality of the theatre or of avoiding naturalistic illusion.[8] Firstly, to avoid naturalism is not necessarily to avoid illusion, or at any rate an adequate conviction of the reality of the fictive events. In the live theatre the non-naturalistic method can actually be a more effective means of enabling the spectator to 'suspend his disbelief' than the naturalistic method, since the spectator is not constantly distracted by the unintentional discrepancies between the stage image and reality it is purporting to counterfeit. The relatively bare set has the advantage of throwing into relief the reality of the people and objects on it and/or of concentrating attention on what is essential to the story being told. It has the further advantage of implicating the spectator in the creation of the fictive reality, for it is through the operation of *his* imagination that the elements of the set and the action are drawn together to form a whole. Brecht praised Neher's decorations for being 'suggestions'. 'They enliven the fantasy of the spectator rather than lame it by excessive detail.' (GW 16, 634) Here, as in other areas of Brecht's theatrical language (such as Weigel's famous 'silent scream' when Mother Courage loses her son Swiss Cheese), Brecht's practice depends fundamentally on the empathetic involvement of the spectator. In fact, without it his alienation effects would have nothing to get any purchase on.

The style of any particular Brechtian *mise-en-scène* was reportedly 'always something arrived at during the last phase of production'.[9] On the other hand there were certain general hallmarks of the Brechtian style to be found in most productions. The sparse set was one, another the even, white light which looked so unaffected but which could take days of special lighting rehearsal and a great deal of electricity to produce. As well as encouraging concentration on the things it exhibited, this lighting made a symbolic contribution to the whole, claiming for the stage that it was the space of reason. The white light permitted other aesthetic effects to flourish, those of colour, for example, or line. Along the front of the stage there usually ran a half-height, unweighted linen curtain that fluttered when opening or closing. Its quality of lightness was one which Brecht held in high esteem and sought to develop in many other areas of the production. In order to impart this quality to the actors' performance after the lengthy, bit-by-bit process of rehearsal, Brecht would arrange, just before the premiere, a 'marking rehearsal' during which the 'actors, not in costumes, but on set, had to walk quickly through all the actions of the show, quoting text very rapidly, without any effort at acting, but keeping the rhythm, the pauses and so on, intact,'; the effect was to make the actors relax, 'memorize every physical detail, and give them a keen sense of the show's rhythmic pattern'.[10] The aesthetic polish and stylistic coherence thereby bestowed on a Brechtian production was yet another of the means whereby Brecht contrived to win the spectator's assent to the epic narrator's sovereign account of the world.

5
Saint Joan of the Stockyards

In 1929 Brecht wrote in an essay 'On Form and Subject Matter' that formal innovation was necessary if the drama was once again to perform the traditional function of major drama (*das große Drama*), which was to confront the public with the central issues of the age. The traditional form of drama, he argued, could no longer encompass the complexities of the modern world where the life of the individual was profoundly affected by events and processes over which he had no direct, personal control, where indeed the individual had become a factor of much less historical significance than anonymous institutions and social classes. How was drama to deal, for example, with an event like the discovery of petroleum?

> Simply to comprehend the new areas of subject-matter imposes a new dramatic and theatrical form. Can we speak of money in the form of iambics? 'The Mark, first quoted yesterday at 50 dollars, now beyond 100, soon may rise, etc' – how about that? Petroleum resists the five-act form; today's catastrophes do not progress in a straight line but in cyclical crises; the 'heroes' change

with the different phases, are interchangeable, etc.; the graph of people's actions is complicated by abortive actions; fate is no longer a single coherent power; rather there are fields of force which can be seen radiating in opposite directions; the power groups themselves comprise movements not only against one another but within themselves, etc., etc. Even to dramatize a simple newspaper report one needs something much more than the dramatic technique of a Hebbel or an Ibsen. This is no boast but a sad statement of fact. It is impossible to explain a present-day character by features, or a present-day action by motives, that would have been adequate in our fathers' time. (BT, p. 30)

Brecht had been developing views of this kind since 1926, and the opera *Rise and Fall of the City of Mahagonny* (1929) had treated contemporary social processes in a symbolic, fantastical manner, but his first play to base itself on real large-scale economic and social processes was *Saint Joan of the Stockyards*, the first version of which was ready for staging (but not actually staged) in 1931. In this play the workings of the capitalist economy are exemplified by a crisis on the Chicago meat-market which leads to the collapse and re-organisation of the market. In the first version of the play these events supposedly take place 'around 1900', but they are of transparent topical relevance to the depression which had deepened in Germany and other parts of Europe in the wake of the Wall Street crash of 1929.

According to a much-quoted analysis by Käthe Rülicke, the events of the play follow the classic capitalist economic cycle of overproduction, crisis, stagnation, resumption of production, as described in Karl Marx's *Capital*, whereby economic power is concentrated at the end of the cycle in

fewer hands than at the beginning.[1] The operation of the
commodities and financial markets, itself a complicated
enough subject to dramatise, is set in a yet wider social
context that includes the masses of the unemployed whose
lives depend on the machinations in the higher spheres of
economic activity, the Salvation Army (or Black Straw
Hats, as they are known in the play) who seek to relieve the
distress of the unemployed with soup and sermons, and the
efforts of class-conscious elements amongst the workers to
organise strike resistance to the plans of the factory-
owners. The ambitious aim of the play is thus to analyse not
only events at what Marx called the 'economic base' of
society but also the relations of such events to the
organisational and cultural 'superstructure' of society.

The action begins with Pierpont Mauler, co-owner of a
beef-processing business, reading the first of a series of
letters from some 'friends in New York' (evidently well-
placed and well-informed men on Wall Street) advising him
to 'take his hand from the beef-trade' because the domestic
market for beef has become glutted and the customs
barriers protecting markets in the South are resisting all
attempts to breach them. Concealing this information,
Mauler offers to sell his share of the business to his partner,
Cridle, on the pretext that he can no longer stand the sight
of animals going to the slaughter. Cridle agrees to take over
Mauler's shares, provided the latter first destroys their
competitor, Lennox. When Mauler fulfills this condition by
a campaign of price-cutting he not only destroys Lennox's
business but also brings down the value of all shares in the
beef-market, including those of his own company. As a
result Cridle cannot raise enough capital to pay for the
shares he has contracted to buy from Mauler. When
accused by Joan Dark, an officer in the Black Straw Hats,
of causing misery to those made unemployed by the vicious

trade war, Mauler is prompted by a mixture of fear of social unrest and ambition to control the whole of the beef-trade, to place orders for canned meat while, at the same time, secretly buying up all available livestock. This puts him in a position to ruin all of his competitors in the canning trade, since they contract to deliver meat to him at prices agreed during a period of slump but are then obliged to buy the necessary livestock *from* him at prices so high that they are bound to go bankrupt. In the process he too goes bankrupt, but only to be hailed subsequently as the saviour of the market when he proposes the formation of a cartel (in which he will hold fifty per cent of the shares) that will stabilise meat production at a level thirty per cent below its previous level and with a work force reduced by thirty per cent.

Applying Brecht's own criteria that art should follow reality and that its purpose is to be informative and educative, *Saint Joan* must be judged to be of little use to any spectator coming to the theatre in search of instruction about economic crises or even about Karl Marx's interpretation of such crises. Firstly, the cycle of boom and slump, as analysed by Marx, results from the impersonal logic of economic processes driven by the capitalist principle of maximising profit. What Brecht portrays, by contrast, is a struggle for domination amongst a group of individual entrepreneurs whose personal motives and qualities – ambition, vengefulness, cleverness or stupidity – crucially affect the course of events.

Brecht's intention thereby was clearly to counter the belief that economic disasters were like natural ones, by demonstrating that economic events were the consequence of human activity that in turn was directed by self-interest. Yet this personalisation of the business principles of competition, profit-maximisation and capital-concentration in a 'conspiracy theory' of economics becomes down-right implausible when translated into dramatic action. Mauler's opening gambit of dumping his shares on Cridle, for example, depends entirely on Cridle being gullible and short-sighted to a degree that is incompatible with his status as co-owner of one of Chicago's largest canning firms. Although he has been Mauler's partner for years, Cridle does not pause even for a moment to ask the obvious and important question why, if Mauler has lived so long with his 'old weakness' for animals, he should suddenly become so upset by the sight of a single ox that he is willing to sell his shares for much less than their current value. Nor does Cridle foresee the entirely predictable consequences for the value of his own investment of a damaging price-war with Lennox.

Each stage in Mauler's eventual take-over of the meat trade rests on the same implausible assumption that all the other businessmen around Mauler lack any insight into the operations of the market or any resourcefulness in counter-ing his manoeuvres. Equally unconvincing is the notion that the entire commodity market in beef can collapse because one individual, Mauler's broker Slift, becomes so carried away with the excitement of 'squeezing the throats' of his competitors that he forces prices up beyond the point the market can stand and thereby causes universal bank-ruptcy. The end of the whole affair makes just as little sense: no explanation is given for the fact that Mauler, bankrupt one minute, is able to finance a majority holding in the cartel the next. Nor is it made clear why new machinery is being installed at a time when it is proposed to cut production by a third. One suspects that the Berliner Ensemble was trying to make a virtue out of necessity when it declared the 'impenetrability' of the economic events to be the central theme of its production of the play in 1968.[2]

Despite Brecht's claim in the essay cited above that the five-act form was unsuited to the task of reflecting contemporary reality, particularly in its economic aspect, this was precisely the form he chose for *Saint Joan of the Stockyards*. In its first completed version the play was divided into five acts and even when, in later versions, this became obscured by the re-numbering of the scenes, the action retains the classic structure of main plot (Mauler's takeover of the meat trade) and counter- or sub-plots (Joan's responses to Mauler's machinations and her various experiences with the unemployed, the Black Straw Hats and the organised workers). In part this choice of form can be explained in terms of a parody of classical drama whereby Brecht sought to discredit the bourgeois cultural superstructure by casting the crude words and actions of real bourgeois in the style traditionally reserved in the theatre for a 'higher' reality, the ideological function of which was to divert the mind from coarse actuality. But the classic form, even as he parodied it, was of enormous help to Brecht in defining what he called the gestic substance (*gestischen Gehalt*) of the socio-economic processes under consideration and in evisaging them 'in an actable perspective' ('*in mimischer Perspektive*'). Before examining Brecht's borrowings from the Classics in any detail we need to consider Brecht's vision of the 'gestic substance' of life under capitalism.

The *Grundgestus* or fundamental character of human relations in the world of the play is one of ruthless exploitation. Exhausted by her vain efforts to ameliorate the condition of the poor in Chicago, the dying Joan Dark reaches the bleak conclusion: 'Only force helps where force rules / Only men help where men are' (SJ, 109). The play prepares the audience for this moral by unremittingly showing the characters either inflicting or suffering all manner of violence – physical, economic, emotional and moral – or trying ineffectually to help the victims of violence. The scenes of the play do not simply contrast gestures of violence and help, they pursue the two forms of behaviour through a variety of permutations, showing, for example, how violence may masquerade as help or as a request for help, or that a request for help, as a sign of weakness, may elicit a violent response, or that it may be necessary to resort to violence in order to help eradicate it.

Thus, in the opening scene, for example, where Mauler disguises his violent intent towards Cridle in a plea for help, and Cridle makes his help (that is the exploitation of Mauler's seeming weakness) dependent on Mauler doing violence to Lennox, a hypothesis is set up: man does not help man in the world of Chicago's slaughterhouses. An antithesis is then introduced when the Black Straw Hats appear amongst the unemployed to bring them warm soup and words of comfort. Yet not only is the help represented by their 'thin soup' quickly shown to be inadequate, the unfolding action makes it clear that the relief work of such organisations benefits the exploiters more than the exploited, for it makes the misery of unemployment just barely tolerable and thereby functions as a prop to the existing system and its institutional violence. This is why the capitalists are so willing to finance the work of the Black Straw Hats. As Joan eventually realises, the only true help for the exploited is to free them from the condition of exploitation so that they are no longer dependent on others more powerful than them for charity – or work. The solution to which Brecht leads his heroine is that help must take the form of revolutionary violence to overthrow a system in which violence is endemic. As he put it in another play from the same period, 'Help and violence form a single whole / And the whole must be changed.' (GW 2, 599)

Saint Joan of the Stockyards

Brecht showed considerable imaginative resourcefulness in devising means to give theatrical and dramatic shape to the pervasively, though not always visibly, antagonistic character of life under capitalism. His method involved the extensive quotation of dramatic works that had become enshrined in the standard repertoire of bourgeois theatre, and their adaptation (*Umfunktionierung*) to serve new aims. The name of Lennox, for example, points to *Macbeth* as one of his models. Brecht had once been asked to produce this play for the Munich Kammerspiele but, daunted by the difficulties, had instead written and directed an adaptation of Marlowe's *Edward the Second*. Yet he remained fascinated by *Macbeth* and, not long before beginning work on *Saint Joan*, cited the sequence of scenes showing Macbeth embroiled in a series of 'bloody but hopeless enterprises' as an example of the 'epic' quality of Shakespearean theatre (GW 15, 117). One can see in Mauler's ruthless pursuit of supreme power in Chicago Brecht's completion of the unfinished commission to bring *Macbeth* onto the contemporary stage. Shakespeare's study of feudal anarchy served to put a theatrical face on the capitalist system of unfettered competition, the rough-neck character of Scottish war-lords finding its contemporary equivalent in the thuggish style of the wholesale butchers of Chicago, while the classic scene of confrontation between two warriors at the head of their respective armies was used to translate into theatrical language diffuse conflicts of economic and social interest.

Brecht was quite eclectic in the choice of models he parodied and thereby adapted to his new subject matter. In the early scenes of the play, for example, the unemployed, angry but impotent, are made to speak in verse forms that recall the lamenting chorus of slaves in Greek tragedy:

Alas!
Hell itself
Shuts its gate in our faces!
We are doomed. Bloody Mauler grips
Our exploiter by the throat and
We are the ones who choke!

[SJ, 6]

Repeatedly the rhythms of Hölderlin's 'Hyperion's Song of Fate' are used to express the falling values of shares or the despair of investors, while the events leading up to the final collapse of the market are made the subject of a lengthy 'teichoscopy', a traditional dramatic device for narrating events, such as battles, which cannot be adequately enacted on-stage.

To a German audience, however, the most easily recognisable objects of Brecht's parody would be the plays of Schiller and Goethe which supplied him with a number of very handy dramaturgical devices. The letter from New York which initiates the action, for example, shows Mauler stepping into the ready-made role of a Schillerian conspirator, while his fateful instruction to his broker Slift to 'act as I would have you do' recalls Elisabeth's treacherous treatment of her secretary, Davison, in *Mary Stuart* (*Maria Stuart*). Mostly, however, the pairing of Mauler with Slift is based on the relation of Faust to Mephistopheles in Goethe's *Faust*, both roles proving useful to represent different aspects of capitalist society; Mauler–Faust personifies the 'eternally striving' will of the entrepreneurial spirit, while Slift–Mephisto exemplifies the covert, indirect methods of acquiring wealth and exercising power beloved of big business.

Joan Dark's role as the idealistic but inexperienced young woman was derived partly from Shaw's *Major*

Barbara, partly from Goethe's *Iphigenia on Tauris* (in which a woman tries to mediate between groups of hostile men), but most extensively, of course, from Schiller's play about Jeanne d'Arc, *The Maid of Orleans*. The amalgam of these parts produced a figure who performs a number of important dramaturgical functions: Joan articulates, albeit imperfectly, the grievances of the unemployed; in her efforts to mediate between capitalists and workers she is made to explore areas of society about which she is initially relatively ignorant, and thereby serves to lead the audience through a learning process with her; although, like Schiller's Maid, a flawed heroine, Joan is a focus of sympathy and a means of intensifying the pathos that plays an essential part in the rhetorical strategy of the play; at the same time her initial aversion to violence and belief in the good will of individuals as the source of social progress served as a critical model not only of Christianity and the German idealist tradition, but more concretely of the social reformist politics of the German Social Democratic Party (which during much of the life of the Weimar Republic attracted more criticism from the Communists than did the Nazis).

To describe Brecht's amalgamation of contemporary subject matter with formal and stylistic devices borrowed from the drama of the past as a technique of alienation is acceptable as far as it goes, but this term should not be allowed to obscure the variety of uses to which he puts this method of composition. Firstly, without such recourse to traditional models of plot-structure and character, however ironically deployed, it would have been difficult for him to translate economic processes into the language of the stage. Secondly, apart from its cognitive value as a means of revealing the links between the bourgeois cultural superstructure and its social practices, the equation of, say,

Mauler with Faust permitted Brecht to pursue particular affective goals. When an unscrupulous figure like Mauler slips, while still speaking in blank verse, from a high stylistic register into a much lower, modern idiom, the effect combines burlesque with satire:

> And were it even thus! Wouldst thou be so bold
> To hack from misery like this your pound of flesh?
> Now, when they're watching for a move
> As lynxes do? I would not be so bold!
>
> [SJ, 32; adapted]

But the rhythm of blank verse can equally well function as an effective expressive vehicle for the raw energy of such as Mauler:

> All right, Graham, now I demand your cans.
> You can stuff yourself into one of them.
> I'll teach you the meat business, you
> Traders! From now on I get paid, and well paid
> For every hoof, every calf from here to Illinois!
>
> [SJ, 70]

Similarly, Joan is given hollow-sounding lines when proclaiming her naive belief in human goodness (for example, 'The ice within their breasts has melted quite'), but when she is filled with the kind of revolutionary wrath of which Brecht approves, the elevated diction can carry a weight of pathos no less than it once did in Schiller's hands:

> And there are two languages, above and below
> And two standards for measuring
> And that which bears a human face
> No longer knows itself.
>
> [SJ, 106]

By such means, then, Brecht sought to control the spectator's emotional responses to the events on stage: by making
the figures sympathetic or antipathetic; by putting the
audience in a position of superiority, or narrowing the
emotional gap between figure and spectator; by reducing
the sense that a figure is a plausible individual (in order to
direct attention beyond the 'persona' on the stage to the
social type or group or attitude he represents), or by
developing a figure's individuality (in order to draw the
spectator into emotional and moral engagement with the
fictive events).

Because the social and economic subject-matter of the
play is unusually complicated (even if it fails to do justice to
the real complexity of the world), the dialogue too often
becomes wordily descriptive, rather than truly 'gestic' or
interactive, as the characters expound the intricacies of the
market for the benefit of the audience. Presumably in an
effort to compensate for this tendency to abstractness,
Brecht used a number of strong, simple staging devices to
convey clearly to the audience the main 'curve' of events.
Joan Dark, for example, is first introduced on stage
wearing the uniform of the Black Straw Hats and proudly
carrying its banner. The banner accompanies her when she
leads the unemployed and the farmers to confront the
factory-owners at the stock-exchange. In a later confrontation with the capitalists, her growing militancy is conveyed
by having her turn the flag upside-down in order to drive
these 'usurers' from the 'temple' or meeting-house.
However, as a result of this action, which loses her
organisation its much-needed patrons, she is forced to hand
back her uniform and take leave of her beloved flag.
Deprived of the shelter, warm clothing and food that 'went
with the job', Joan's understanding of the poor grows as she
shares with them the experience of being cold and hungry

on the streets of Chicago. In the end, having failed to help them by not delivering a crucial letter during the strike, Joan's insights into class-warfare make her reject utterly the conciliatory gospel she had once preached. Now the flag is used to underline her development in a fiercely ironic manner as the other Black Straw Hats smother her protests and hide her emaciated body beneath a pile of the brand new banners the organisation has acquired through its pact with the capitalists of Chicago.

Brecht's idea of using the Chicago slaughterhouses both as an example and as a metaphor of capitalist exploitation opened a rich vein of verbal and visual imagery. The chorus of the unemployed and unorganised workers protest at being treated like cattle by the factory owners ('Do you think we are going to stand here like steers?' (SJ, 5)); yet their own passivity and hopelessness, as they vaguely realise, *is* that of a domesticated herd: 'Here are your steers, you butchers.' Such imagery (and a related set that equates the workers with the machinery they operate) reflects Brecht's belief that the capitalist system exploits the productivity of the working classes with the same ruthlessness as it does the resources of the natural world. In one particularly grotesque example, taken from a novel by Upton Sinclair, of the interchangeability of man and animal within the capitalist production process, a worker who falls into the slaughtering plant ends up as 'Uncle Sliced Bacon' in cans!

Anticipating *Animal Farm*, Brecht applied the same bestial imagery to the butcher-capitalists, for example, 'Somewhere some swine is buying everything up' (SJ, 52), or 'thus / Do buffaloes, fighting for grass, trample to shreds the grass they fight for'. (SJ, 16) Brecht also teased out a thread of motifs from another element in the central slaughterhouse conceit, the imagery of food and eating

1. First entry of the wagon. Courage's sons work like carthorses while she relaxes and sings (see p. 103). *Mother Courage and her Children*, Berliner Ensemble, 1951.

2. Mother Courage is lured behind the wagon to sell a buckle; Eiliff is lured away to sell himself to the army (see p. 96). *Mother Courage and her Children*, Berliner Ensemble, 1951.

3. End of Scene 1: having "mislaid" Eiliff, Mother Courage must herself push the wagon. A soldier points out the moral directly to the audience (see p. 97). *Mother Courage and her Children*, Berliner Ensemble, 1951.

4. The "domestication" of war. Dumb Kattrin dreams of love in the clothes of a whore (see p. 104). *Mother Courage and her Children*, Berliner Ensemble, 1951.

5. Kattrin, bandaged after an attack by a soldier, pulls the wagon. Her mother sings in praise of war and trade (see p. 102). *Mother Courage and her Children*, Berliner Ensemble, 1951.

6. Courage's last exit (see p. 104). *Mother Courage and her Children*, Berliner Ensemble, 1951.

7. Three Gods arrive in Szechwan, bourgeois figures visiting the world of the poor (see p. 140). *The Good Person of Szechwan*, Berliner Ensemble, 1957.

8. The Gods' sixth visit to Wang. A black eye illustrates their reception by mortals (see p. 148). *The Good Person of Szechwan*, Berliner Ensemble, 1957.

9. At the end of *The Good Person of Szechwan* the Gods depart on a rosy cloud, abandoning Shen Teh to her dilemma (see p. 148). *The Good Person of Szechwan*, Berliner Ensemble, 1957.

10. Shen Teh in her natural state, with unmasked face, open, relaxed gestures and soft clothing. *The Good Person of Szechwan*, Berliner Ensemble, 1957.

11. Shen Teh's "cousin", Shui Ta, with hard mask, tightly buttoned suit and angular gestures. *The Good Person of Szechwan*, Berliner Ensemble, 1957.

12. The alienation of humanity: members of the ruling class in *The Caucasian Chalk Circle*, wearing hard, cruel masks and heavy clothes (see p. 172). *The Caucasian Chalk Circle*, Berliner Ensemble, 1955.

13. Gruscha bids farewell to Simon. Contrasts of texture underpin the argument: the softness of flesh with the hardness of armour (see p. 172). *The Caucasian Chalk Circle*, Berliner Ensemble, 1955.

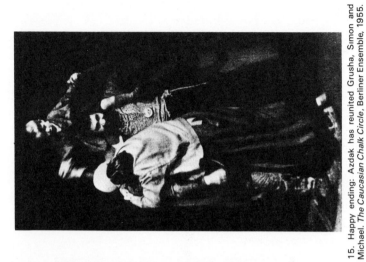

14. Grusha hears the child calling to her (see p. 162). Facial expression and gesture invite empathetic understanding. *The Caucasian Chalk Circle*, Berliner Ensemble, 1955.

15. Happy ending: Azdak has reunited Grusha, Simon and Michael. *The Caucasian Chalk Circle*, Berliner Ensemble, 1955.

which lent itself particularly well to 'gestic' realisation (whereas the animal imagery translated more easily into stage-design). The play as a whole seeks to jolt the audience into grasping the scandalous paradox that the same capitalist mode of production that produces vast surpluses of food also condemns many of the producers to suffer hunger periodically – while at the same time burning the surplus that could feed them. Throughout the play, scene after scene focuses on food, eating, greed, hunger, on well-fed 'butchers' and the thin figures of the unemployed in order to spell out in concrete terms the simple facts about a complicated system.

The theme is kept to the forefront of attention through the experiences of Joan Dark. From her very first appearance on stage she is associated with food as she ladles out soup to the unemployed, only to complain of their ingratitude and lack of concern for 'higher' values: 'That sort won't raise its mind above the edge of a bowl.' Step by step she is made to lose the haughty attitude of the well-fed to the material facts of life, as she sees how easily the poor can be blackmailed by hunger, and then, having been expelled from the Black Straw Hats, experiences hunger personally. Each stage is given clear theatrical expression: the desperate gesture of Frau Luckerniddle as she begins to eat the food that is to be her reward for keeping silent about the fate of her husband (the worker who fell into the boiling-vat) becomes Joan's own when, after a week without food, she visits Mauler. Because Mauler refuses to re-open the factories, however, Joan feels she has to stop eating his food, and pushes the plate away. This gesture of rejecting food is then repeated in the last scene when the Black Straw Hats make a show of 'helping' the emaciated Joan (and thereby silencing her denunciation of the capitalists), by spooning into her mouth the same thin soup

83

as she had dispensed to the unemployed at the beginning of the play.

Although he considered it an important work, Brecht never directed a 'model' production of *Saint Joan* such as exists for *Mother Courage* or *The Mother*. Perhaps rather surprisingly, he gave the opportunity to direct the first stage production of the play to Gustav Gründgens who had written asking for permission to stage it in 1932, just before the accession to power of Hitler and Brecht's departure from Germany (where Gründgens, by contrast, continued to work throughout the years of National Socialist rule). Brecht's reply to his request in 1949, on his return from exile to the GDR, presumably came as an embarrassment to Gründgens in the years of tension between the two Germanies, for he did not take advantage of Brecht's consent until 1959, three years after Brecht's death, when he produced it at the Hamburg Schauspielhaus.

The success of Gründgens' production with the very bourgeois audiences whose manipulative and exploitative practices the play was written to expose, was attributed by a number of commentators to the fact that Gründgens had emasculated the political message of the play by removing provocative references to Bolshevism or to the Communist alternative to the chaos of Capitalism. Gründgens evidently interpreted the play in a generalising, unhistorical manner, so that it became a bitter melancholy reflection on the fate of spirituality and goodness, represented by the heroine, in a coarsely materialistic world generally populated by marionettes and megalomaniacs. Yet despite its alleged failure to do justice to the political intentions of the dramatist, this production had the benefit of being designed by Brecht's oldest and closest collaborator, Caspar Neher, and explored the theatrical possibilities of the play along lines that have influenced subsequent directors and designers.

Even before the action proper began, Neher's design drew for its effects on the vast playing area of the Schauspielhaus stage, presenting the waiting audience with an empty stage open on all sides to reveal the machinery normally kept hidden behind curtains. As the house-lights dimmed, the machinery rattled into operation, screens were hoisted and banners dropped into position, painted in colours which, though not blood-coloured in any obvious way, 'had the reek of blood about them', while above the set there hung, like a double-headed eagle, an emblem of two ox-heads. The designer's exploitation of the size of the stage suited the play in a number of respects. The large format of the set was in tune with the claim of the play to represent, in the tradition of the medieval and baroque theatres, a whole world – 'this world, resembling a slaughterhouse', as Joan remarks when she enters it for the first time; the suggestion was reinforced by the turning of the turntable stage.

That Brecht had indeed intended to allude ironically to this tradition of Christian drama is indicated by the many instances of cosmic imagery in the text (equating the laws of the market with the laws of planetary movement), by the constant references to the vertical order of relationships within capitalism, by the echo of the 'harrowing of Hell' in Joan's thrice-repeated 'descent to the depths', by Mauler's God-like power to bring down the edifice of the capitalist world and re-erect it again in seven days. Neher carried through the parody in his design, keeping the stage bare, open and cheerless, in contrast to the elaborate baroque stage which had celebrated, by way of analogy, the splendour and mystery of the world-stage, and only once quoting baroque pomp directly, in the last scene, where the rear of the stage was dominated by the new organ gifted to the mission-house by the capitalists, a floodlit, gleaming monster in gold and silver. By the same token, whereas the baroque stage had concealed the machinery that effected its theatrical miracles, Neher left the machinery plainly visible and audible as a sign that the capitalist world of 'ordered disorder', far from being as mysterious as the Divine Creation, is the product of human, self-interested contrivance. Neher's minimalist sets – some corrugated-iron sheets here, panels of mahogany there – functioned as 'signposts through a sequence of events, the true meaning of which is to be sought "behind" the play itself'.[3]

Just as there is a stylistic divergence in Brecht's text between the burlesque manner generally used in the scenes centred on the business world and the rising tone of pathos associated with Joan, a divergence which produces an effect of extreme emotional-aesthetic dissonance when the two styles are brought together in the scene of Joan's death and canonisation, so Neher and Gründgens varied their style of staging in different scenes. A classicistic temple façade hung above the scenes played on the stock-exchange where dealers gestured like Shakespearean peers, brandishing their umbrellas like swords, their open coats revealing gold and silver waistcoats like chainmail, their movements stylised by the director in balletic or pantomimic manner. In the later scenes showing Joan on the streets near the slaughterhouses, by contrast, the emotional impact was intensified by creating, with the aid of a wind-machine and specially angled lighting, the effect of a driving blizzard. The image of Joan bent against the storm remained in the memory, typifying for a number of critics Gründgens' conception of the character as the embodiment of frail humanity in a gross and hostile world.

Gründgens was helped in creating this impression by the physical qualities of Hanne Hiob (Brecht's daughter by his first marriage) in the part of Joan, for her fragile-seeming figure (and pretty, soulful face) contrasted starkly with the butchers and cattle-men into whose world she incautiously enters. The physical bulk of these men was emphasised by their style of dress, uniform for each group: wide-brimmed stetsons and padded shoulders for the farmers, bowlers, black morning-coats and trousers with unusually broad stripes for the businessmen. Such suggestive visual contrasts were entirely typical of Brecht's own staging methods, particularly in plays where he wanted to bring out the effect of parable. No doubt Brecht would have sought to maintain a more critical view of Joan in the storm-scenes where Gründgens emphasised the pathos, but Gründgens cannot be accused of importing melodrama into the play; he was simply, albeit rather too simply, responding to an important element in the overall emotional economy of the play and one which it shares with the majority of Brecht's plays.

Gründgens' emphasis on Joan's soulful frailty and his failure to develop her angry determination to combat injustice was blamed for making implausible her conduct in the final scene where she calls for the very violence to which she was once so opposed. However, the fault was not all Gründgens', for it is extremely difficult to imagine the Joan of the opening scenes ever being able to utter some of the lines Brecht gives her at the end:

> Therefore, anyone down here who says there is a God
> When none can be seen
> A God who can be invisible and yet help them
> Should have his head knocked on the pavement
> Until he croaks.   (SJ, 108)

Here Brecht's need for a mouthpiece to preach the moral he thought ought to be drawn from the action simply overrode considerations of psychological probability. In earlier parts of the play, too, Joan's behaviour too clearly shows signs of having been manipulated to suit the exigencies of the author's rhetorical design. Thus she must be sufficiently intelligent and concerned with getting to the truth of things for her instantly to see through Slift's attempts to blame the misery of the poor on their viciousness, and yet be gullible enough to relapse, at a late stage in her political development, into her earlier naive trust in individual goodness. Whereas the subordination of individual development to the didactic requirement of reinforcing a lesson through repeated demonstration is more or less acceptable in a 'learning play' like *The Decision* it is likely to be counter-productive in a play for the general public.

Similar problems exist with the character of Mauler. Hermann Schomburg, whose physical bulk suited the part well, was the most praised actor in Gründgens' Hamburg production, but the various critics might almost have been watching different interpretations of the role, so divergent were their views on his handling of it. One commentator, who generally felt that Gründgens had blunted the cutting edge of the satire, saw in Schomburg's Mauler too much 'rosy bonhomie' that obscured the dangerousness of the type[4]; a second considered that Schomburg had lent Mauler 'the most beautiful butcher's face in the world, cunning and brutal'[5]; a third found that Schomburg had made him believe that even a hard man like Mauler was genuinely capable of soft-heartedness and remorse[6]; a fourth admired the way Schomburg had shown Mauler's sentimentality to be something that he had long grown accustomed to, merely something to be coquettish about.[7] It seems likely that each critic had in mind one particular scene or another at the moment of writing his review, for the character obeys the dictates, not of psychological plausibility, but of Brecht's argument as it veers between presenting an allegory of an impersonal large-scale process and showing how individual behaviour supports the capitalist system. Thus Mauler is by turns a satirical version of 'Faustian man', striving for ever greater economic power and only too ready to bear the burden of guilt that this entails, and an individual trapped in a system of exploitation that revolts him. Brecht believed that men necessarily live *with* and *by* contradiction, but he did not succeed in this play in demonstrating convincingly through his dramatic characters *how* contradictions can be lived with.

One of the ways in which critics felt that Gründens' production had sabotaged Brecht's intentions was by the smooth, rapid, film-like flow he imparted to the action. This, some felt, had the effect of emphasising its farcical quality at the cost of didactic pointedness. On the other hand there were some who felt that the fast tempo kept the action lively. Where satire was involved Brecht himself favoured a rapid pace, as in *Drums in the Night* (particularly Act III) or *A Man's a Man*. Other directors who have tackled the allegorising type of parable to which *Saint Joan* belongs have also had recourse to a rapid tempo, possibly to offset the tendency of the dialogue to get bogged down in lengthy expositions of the economic or historical background to events. When the Berliner Ensemble played *Arturo Ui* at breakneck speed this was not felt to be damaging to the play's argument, whereas Alexander Lang's highly polished 1984 production of *Round Heads and Pointed Heads* at the Deutsches Theater in East Berlin has encountered similar objections to those met by Gründgens in Hamburg. On the other hand, not to force the pace or play up the elements of farce is to run the opposite danger, as did the Ensemble's well-designed but strait-laced production of *Saint Joan* in 1968, of having as little appeal to the public as Joan's wordy sermons and watery soup.

6
Mother Courage and her Children

Written on the eve of the Second World War, while Brecht was living in exile in Scandinavia, *Mother Courage and her Children* was intended as a reminder that it is not possible to play with fire without getting burnt. The place of its composition fed into the play in a number of ways. The need to give such warning was borne in on Brecht by his perception that the Scandinavians were prepared to collaborate with Hitler's preparations for war in the expectation of profit and in the mistaken belief that they would not be among Hitler's victims. The moral of the play – that 'you need a big pair of scissors to make a cut from a war' (CM, 68) – had particular relevance to Germany's less powerful Northern neighbours, as did its setting in the Thirty Years War (1618–1648), a war in which Scandinavian countries (particularly Sweden) were embroiled and which cost Europe dearly in both life and property.

Scandinavian history also supplied one of the models for the play's protagonist, in the person of Lotta Svärd, a Swedish cantinière celebrated in popular imagination for her loyal, motherly care towards the soldiers of the regiment in which her beloved had once served. What is most significant about the influence of the Scandinavian background on the play, however, is its contradictory character, arising from the mixture of historical memories it supplied. Although Brecht's Mother Courage is a much less romantically seen figure than the Lotta Svärd in Johan Runeberg's ballad, she retains enough of Lotta's positive qualities for the play to make a more complicated statement about war than the straightforward indictment of the link between profiteering and warmongering on which many of Brecht's statements about the play concentrate.

In comparison with Brecht's preference for relatively direct didacticism in the plays of the early 1930s, in *Saint Joan of the Stockyards*, say, or *The Mother*, where the central characters undergo a (more or less exemplary) learning process that makes explicit the lessons to be learned by the audience, *Mother Courage* approaches its educative task in a new, rather more oblique way. As such, it is the best known of a group of plays, written between the late 1930s and the mid-1940s, which are now regarded as Brecht's classic works. In these plays he drew together elements of his work that had previously tended to operate separately, with the result that the realistic sketches of contemporary life in *Fear and Misery of the Third Reich*, for example, were weakened dramatically by the lack of an overall structure, while the parabolic cohesiveness of *Saint Joan* or *Round Heads and Pointed Heads* was achieved at the cost of realism in situation and character. At the same time

Brecht now placed a new trust in the complexity of the spectator's theatrical experience as the source of his enlightenment. Thus, although Mother Courage frequently makes acute observations about the way war affects people like herself, she remains incorrigible to the end in her attachment to the war. Brecht's intention was not, of course, to make a pessimistic statement about man's inability to learn from experience (although a number of commentators have regarded this as the real, if unintended, truth expressed by the play), but to enable the spectator to gain the kind of historical conspectus of her situation that Courage, caught up in the thick of things, cannot sustain. One of his principal means of doing this was to expose the contradictions in Mother Courage's experiences, another was to incorporate these contradictions in patterns of irony.

   Mother Courage is a dialectically conceived figure. In other words, both she and the situations she finds herself in are systematically built on contradiction. Earning her living as a 'sutler' or camp-follower who provisions the soldiery, Mother Courage occupies a contradictory class position. Her 'crime' in seeking out the war in order to profit from it ('I can't wait till the war is good enough to come to Bamberg') is that of the capitalist class (at that time a rising class, according to the Marxist interpretation of history). On the other hand, as a small trader – and businesses do not come much smaller than hers – she is also one of the common people who simply have to survive as best they can in the social and economic system of their times. This class ambiguity underlies the most obvious contradiction in her life, that between her trade and her role as mother. As Brecht put it, 'The trader-mother became a great, living contradiction.' (CM, 94). She embodies, as it were, the class-struggle in her own person, for whenever she acts as a 'capitalist', seizing some opportunity for profit, she invariably damages her interest as a member of the exploited classes, or, more particularly, as the mother of children who belong to that group. The fate of the family illustrates the fundamental contradiction of war – that it 'renders human virtues deadly, even for those who possess them' (CM, 130), and shows this in turn to be the outcome of the harsh logic of class-society, by virtue of which the productivity of ordinary people is turned into a force that operates against their own interests.

Courage's ambiguous social position enabled Brecht to give her the function of articulating many of his own criticisms of war and especially of the class-interests he saw underlying it. Because her own involvement in the war is purely mercenary she is well-placed to perceive the material interests behind all high-sounding justifications for war:

> To go by what the big shots say, they're waging war for almighty God and in the name of everything that's good and lovely. But look closer, they ain't so silly, they're waging it for what they can get. Else little folk like me wouldn't be in it at all.

> (5ii, 27)

On the other hand, her willingness to tell the unvarnished truth is motivated by the fact that, although she has her wagon, she and her family belong to the mass of ordinary folk whose lives are ruined by the politics of the powerful: 'The best thing for us is when politics get bogged down solid' (5ii, 31).

That men are indeed mostly motivated by concern for their own material and physical well-being is confirmed again and again in the course of the play. Religion is

regarded by all ranks as an irrelevance or an embarrassment, 'piety' is used to justify cruelty, but scorned as soon
as it represents an obstacle to enjoying the spoils of war.
Even as the great Field Marshall Tilly is being carried to his
grave with full military pomp, his soldiers are interested
only in using the opportunity to enjoy a rest, a smoke and a
brandy. Mother Courage's challenge to the official version
of the war is supported by the voice of the playwright, who,
in the texts introducing each scene, counterpoints the
major events that are represented in history books with the
minor events that are in fact of much greater significance in
the lives of ordinary folk: 'Tilly's victory at Leipzig costs
Mother Courage four officers' shirts' (5ii, 48).

With her wit, perceptiveness and ability to bamboozle
figures of authority, Mother Courage is cast in the mould of
Jaroslav Hasek's 'Good Soldier Schwejk'. To the extent
that she presents, in an appealing manner, a critical view of
war that Brecht himself endorsed, the playwright is still
using direct rhetorical methods to shape the opinions of the
audience. However, Mother Courage is far from being an
unambiguously positive heroine, and irony plays a large part
in making this plain. The audience is encouraged to criticise
the war with Mother Courage, but also to develop a critical
view of her attitudes and behaviour. In fact, Mother
Courage's very perceptiveness contributes importantly to
the ironic presentation of her fate.

An ironic tone is established as soon as the play begins,
for the first thing with which the audience is confronted
is a projected text (a modern descendent of the 'naive'
Shakespearean device of simply announcing the place and
time of the action), telling them that a recruiting campaign
is going on and that 'A son of the sutler Anna Fierling,
known under the name of Mother Courage, gets mislaid'.[1]
Apart from the flat, dead-pan tone, the irony emerges in

the odd way of describing the loss of a son as if he were some object, like a walking stick. This verbal hint is then picked up by a whole series of images in the scene that follows which put human beings on the same level as animals and objects of use, for example: 'Takes a war to get proper nominal rolls and inventories – shoes in bundles and corn in bags, and man and beast properly numbered and carted off, 'cause it stands to reason: no order, no war.' (5ii, 6) Here the irony is laid on so thickly that the corporal's eulogy of wartime order takes on the quality of verbal farce, an effect heightened by the fact that, as he recites it, he is freezing in the April wind, an eloquent example of the miserable reality of war for the men on the ground.

When first introduced into this context, Mother Courage appears to be a master of irony rather than its object. The corporal and recruiting officer are determined to recruit her sons, but it seems at first that Mother Courage is so much more alert and in control of each situation that the recruiters are as likely to fail here as they have elsewhere. Yet by the end of the scene, despite her quick-witted handling of the situation (she knows what the recruiters are up to, and seeks to deflect them by a whole series of tactical ploys), she has become the victim of irony, when one of her own initial tactics rebounds on her. Early in the confrontation she tries to distract the 'gentlemen officers' by offering to sell them a pistol or buckle. When the threat to her sons seems to be past, and Courage has climbed eagerly back on to the wagon, the Recruiting Officer in turn distracts *her*, simply by suggesting that the corporal should take a look at the buckle after all. After only the briefest hesitation (and at great risk to the psychological plausibility of the scene) Mother Courage climbs down again and allows herself to be drawn into conversation on one side of the wagon while on the other the officer signs up her son, Eilif, who is all too eager to exchange the harness of a cart-horse for the uniform of a soldier. Whereas Mother Courage came on to the stage seated, on the wagon, with her daughter Kattrin by her side, she has to continue her journey on foot, with the wagon being pulled by Kattrin and her remaining brother.

Not only is this opening scene structured ironically, it also serves as the starting point of a longer ironic curve that stretches from the first to the last scene, holding together a loose sequence of incidents which are not bound into the traditional dramatic structure of action and counter-action between protagonist and antagonist. Just as Baal's ubiquitous, but hidden antagonist was Death, Mother Courage's is the war. Like him, she will eventually be defeated. To make us expect this outcome from the outset, Brecht builds into his play very familiar ironic structures such as the association of pride with a fall, insight with blindness, greatness with a tragic flaw or error. That Anna Fierling has a greater stature than most people is indicated by her by-name; that she is both wise and stupid, insightful and blind is evident from the events leading up to the loss of Eilif; that she is proud is evident from her response to the corporal's sarcastic remark that hers is 'a nice family': 'Aye, me cart and me have seen the whole world' (5ii, 7). Subsequent scenes pick up these motifs so that events are perceived as parts of a coherent whole. Courage's moments of insight, for example, are juxtaposed with examples of blindness: immediately after a scene where Courage curses the war because of the harm it has done to her daughter, she is seen, once more astride a well-loaded wagon, pulled by the bandaged Kattrin, singing the praises of the war.

It is part of Brecht's irony to give to Mother Courage herself the function of announcing the bleak pattern to be completed by the action, when, in the opening scene, she pretends to foretell the future. By requiring first the recruiters and then her own children to draw black crosses from a helmet she hopes to frighten and distract the soldiers, and to intimidate Eilif, whose boldness she fears will draw him into soldiering. Yet what she foretells comes about. By the end of the opening scene she has already lost Eilif to the army. By the end of the play her own actions will have (directly or indirectly) brought upon her children the very fate which, by pretending to predict it, she had intended to prevent.

In one sense, the pattern completed by the action is a moral one: Mother Courage's hubris in believing that *she* can bring *her* family safely through the war, regardless of whatever else it may destroy, is 'punished' by the loss, one by one, of all her children. The moral thus exemplified is announced, not at the end of the play, but at the end of the first scene: 'Like the war to nourish you? / Have to feed it something too' (5ii, 13). This moral pattern is reinforced by the fates of other characters: the whore Yvette, initially an attractive girl, enjoys material success when she becomes the mistress of an old colonel, but pays for this by the loss of her physical attractiveness and human warmth. Eilif is at first rewarded for his cunning and cruelty, but a similar 'brave' action, done during an *apparent* cessation of hostilities, leads to his execution.

Yet the play as a whole does not encourage a morally smug response. Courage's other son, Swiss Cheese, is also executed, but he is a gentle, rather stupid soul whose only fault is excessive honesty and a sense of duty. Kattrin, kindly and so fond of children that she ultimately lays down her life to save the children of Halle, repeatedly and innocently falls victim to the barbarity of soldiers. The fates of Swiss Cheese and Kattrin *can* be drawn into the moral pattern of guilt and punishment by seeing them as victims of their mother's guilt, for she haggles so long over the sale of her wagon that she fails to save Swiss Cheese from execution, while Kattrin receives the mutilating injury that destroys any possibility of marriage and children of her own while away doing a business errand for her mother. But the moral case against Mother Courage also reveals an objective crux in her life. Certainly, the harm done to her children is associated with her business dealings. These business dealings, however, are the means by which she attempts to fulfil a mother's obligation to provide for her family. Mother Courage haggles long over the price of the wagon because she knows that, if the sale produces no more than the bribe needed to save Swiss Cheese, she and her children will be left destitute in the midst of war. Equally, she depends on Kattrin's contribution to the business that feeds the pair of them. That Mother Courage is not at bottom uncaring, or malicious towards her family is evident throughout, from her willingness to defend them with a knife from the recruiters in the opening scene, from her grief for the dead Swiss Cheese, from her refusal, even when near starvation, to abandon Kattrin in order to follow the cook to Utrecht. Ironically, this decision does not save Kattrin, because the girl's frustrated desire for children (frustrated by the mutilations she has received while in the care of her own mother) makes her prepared to sacrifice her life in an attempt to save the city of Halle.

Taking together all these elements – the heroine's great personal qualities and her blindness, her pride and her fall, her guilt and her suffering, the subjective errors and the objective coercion – it is evident that the ironic organisation of the whole serves not only to illuminate events intellectually, but also to cast Courage's life in the mould of tragedy. Repeatedly, she is made the object of a complex mix of emotions, not only of anger and outrage but also of fear and pity – as she sits by Kattrin's side waiting to hear if Swiss Cheese will be reprieved, or even as she strides along, singing the praises of war, seemingly oblivious of Kattrin's bandaged face, an emblem of past and probably future suffering. Courage is no monster but a fallible human being, whose failings are both part of her humanity and fostered by circumstances. She is tempted to live in a way that destroys herself and her family because the world she inhabits is so organised that the natural urge to provide for oneself is forced into destructive and ultimately self-destructive channels.

Tragedy, as the form forced on life by historical contingency, was not something that Brecht in practice entirely excluded from his Epic Theatre – provided that it stimulated a determination to eradicate the causes of suffering. On the other hand, it was a chancy experiment which could backfire if the painful experiences the audience is made to share were divorced in its reception of the play from a clear insight into the objective historical conditions that seduced to blindness, maimed lives and produced pain. Here Brecht relied heavily on the double function of irony, as a generator both of insight and pathos, to create a form of tragedy that not only faced up to the painful complexity of man's historically conditioned existence but also sought to offer something more than a mere counsel of despair.

After experimenting with the *Antigone* adaptation in Chur and with *Mr Puntila* in Zürich, the production of *Mother Courage* that opened at the Deutsches Theater in East Berlin in January 1949 was Brecht's greatest opportunity so far to put into practice his ideas about production and acting and to discover whether both plays and ideas would stand up to the demands of actual theatrical performance. In the event, the enormous success of this production (which led to the establishment of the Berliner

Ensemble) and of the variants he developed over a number of years with different casts and in different theatres, proved that his writing and his theatrical ideas were eminently practicable and effective. *Mother Courage* became one of the foremost models of powerful, living theatre in the post-war period.

This outcome was achieved because Brecht's theatrical practice was a good deal more flexible than some of his theoretical statements, particularly those made at the beginning of the 1930s, had suggested it would be. Brecht's theatre 'worked' largely because of his unremitting insistence that the full sensuous resources of the medium (or media) of theatre should be employed to put flesh on to the skeleton of the *Fabel*. In practice Brecht did not direct his plays so as to produce intellectual *rather than* emotional theatre. His notes on his *Theaterarbeit* (theatre work) naturally tend to stress the point that was being made by this arrangement or that detail because it was this emphasis on the argumentative, demonstrative function of theatre that gave his work its peculiar character in relation to other available forms of theatre. However it is quite clear, both from his own record of work and from the actual effect of his productions on audiences, that the result was not dry didacticism. In fact, if anything, his problem was that his productions packed so much emotional punch that, despite all his intensive intellectual input, audiences and critics left the theatre deeply affected but not necessarily in agreement about what it was they were supposed to have learned from the experience. The following account of his staging will both describe the ways he used the resources of the theatre to persuade the audience to take a particular view of Mother Courage's experiences, and attempt to explain why the actual effect of the play in performance diverged from what he intended.

The design of Mother Courage's covered wagon, something 'half-way between a military vehicle and a general
store' (5ii, 102), was taken over by Brecht from Teo Otto's
designs for the first production of the play in Zürich in
1943, as was much of the blocking of the scenes, which
naturally was closely bound up with the position and
functions of the wagon. The wagon is on stage in ten out of
the twelve scenes of the play (the exceptions are Scene 2,
played in a Captain's tent and kitchen, and Scene 4, played
in front of an officer's tent). It is used to convey 'narratorial' information of a materialist nature that is intended to
explain (in accordance with the Marxist tenet that consciousness is determined by the material conditions of life)
the behaviour of the characters, particularly that of Mother
Courage. When the wagon first trundles on to the stage at
the beginning of the Thirty Years War its new awning and a
freshly-painted sign correspond to Courage's keen spirit of
enterprise as she pursues a new opportunity for profit.
When the wagon leaves the stage (twelve years later) its
tattered and battered state not only reflects the disappoint-
ment of her material ambitions but also suggests her
spiritual reduction to a state of bare, desperate determination to struggle on. When, in between, the wagon is hung
with a wide variety of goods, we are invited to see the
connection between the fact that she is 'now at the peak of
her business career' and her cynical, devil-may-care defence of war (in words that echo and parody Clausewitz's
definition of war as politics conducted by other means):
'But what is war but private trading/That deals in blood
instead of boots' (5ii, 60). As she sings the wagon is pulled
by Kattrin, her disfigured face swathed in bandages.

The wagon is thus a powerful device for tracing a
coherent development in the various episodes that befall
Courage and her family over a long period of time. It also

creates the impression of a unity of place, for, although the locations of the play constantly change as the family follows the armies up and down Europe for twelve years, the scene of the action is almost invariably the space around the wagon. This scenic focus is one of Brecht's most effective means of subverting the 'official' view of history, since it insists that the measure of history is its effects on the limited domestic sphere on which the lives of common people are centred. At the same time as it asserts the little man's right to concern himself primarily with the banal business of everyday life, however, this scenic arrangement implies criticism of such political apathy by showing the recurrent disruption of the domestic sphere by events decided elsewhere. By constantly showing life in the perspective of people who are the passive 'objects of history', the play implicitly raises the question of why they do not make themselves into the active 'subjects of history'. However, in order to perceive this, particularly in relation to a historical period in which the common man's scope for political action was virtually non-existent, the spectator would already need to have the political awareness the play seeks to develop. Indeed, Brecht was criticised in Communist circles because of the alleged absence from the play of the 'idea of the revolutionary critical transformation of the world'. (CM, 86)

Above all, the wagon gives concrete, visual expression to the 'great living contradiction' Courage embodies as businesswoman and mother. It is at one and the same time a place of refuge and relaxation, a territory to be defended, the price she pays for Swiss Cheese's life, and a source of sustenance for the family. It is also used to clarify the 'gestic' (that is, relational) substance of events. Thus, although the wagon is a means of sustaining the *whole* family, when it first appears it is being pulled by her two

103

sons, while Courage and her daughter ride on top. Relations within the family are thereby shown also to be relations of exploitation – which partly explains why Eilif is so keen to seek his fortune as a soldier. In the opening scene the wagon halts near the front of the stage, somewhat off-centre, so as to mark off distinctly family from soldiers, the intended prey from the hunters. The soldiers then try a variety of ploys to invade the family 'territory'. When they eventually succeed in separating the mother and one member of her family, by tempting each of them with the prospect of personal gain, the wagon ironically provides the means of driving a wedge between mother and children. The family 'fortress' has thus been transformed into – or revealed to be – a trap.

There is a multitude of such examples of the wagon being used to show, in a manner that is theatrically forceful but not forced, what Marxist analysis defines as the power of the material conditions of life to alienate man from his own humanity. When Mother Courage is shown in the final scene, old, bent double, pulling the heavy wagon alone, on the seemingly endlessly revolving stage (Brecht deliberately made her walk-off last much longer than the audience is at first prepared for), the wagon is used to make the point to great pathetic effect. Yet it also makes points comically, as in the scene where it supports one end of a washing line, the other end of which is tethered to a cannon. Here the domestication even of war is both a tribute to man's tenacious ability to get on with the business of living by adapting to whatever situation he finds himself in, and (seen retrospectively, in the light of the family's destruction) a symptom of the deadly habituation which allows untenable conditions to be sustained. From these few examples alone, it should be apparent that, at its best, Brecht's art of theatre consisted of creating scenes that were both intellectually *and* emotionally telling, and that these effects were clearly designed to reinforce each other.

In order to create the most favourable conditions for the intensive exploitation of major stage properties, such as Mother Courage's wagon, Brecht favoured an otherwise uncluttered stage and even, white lighting – 'As much of it as our equipment permitted' (5ii, 99). The effect of the concentration produced by surrounding a central object with empty space is naturally the greater, the larger the stage. At the Deutsches Theater in 1949 Brecht had the advantage of working on a vast stage, the depth of which was further emphasised by the use of a semi-circular backdrop or 'cyclorama'. The grey tones of the set, combined with the huge empty space, naturally had a powerfully suggestive effect on audiences in bomb-flattened Berlin in 1949. At the other end of the scale, great attention was paid to matters of detail. Helene Weigel used a handful of carefully selected properties in a variety of ways to help tell the story of Courage, her children and her wagon. In her lapel she wore a large metal spoon, badge of her dual functions as mother and victualler. To focus attention on the importance of business dealings in Courage's life, Weigel found a purse with a particularly loud click. Even when paying for Kattrin's funeral, Weigel–Courage counted out a sum of money and then, seemingly absent-mindedly, put one of the coins back in the purse. A chain of silver coins worn around the character's neck simultaneously connoted vanity, enslavement and, possibly, the thirty silver pieces paid to Judas for his treachery.

The acting of Helene Weigel, was by common consent, one of the main reasons for the 'unforgettable' quality of the Berlin production of *Courage*. According to the account by Friedrich Luft (nowadays Berlin's senior theatre critic), Weigel's performance was epic in the manner prescribed by Brecht:

> An acting *tour de force* which she achieved without any apparent effort (. . .) Standing, as it were, intelligently *beside* her role, she presented the fate of this woman caught up in the war, without losing her own identity in that of the character. In her playing she made an example of the character, with a mimetic persuasiveness that seemed to be the most natural thing in the world. How she did all this is something that needs to be studied more closely and analysed on the basis of repeated observation. There is an expressive force at work here which was new and frequently took one's breath away.[2]

Weigel's acting technique was reportedly 'restrained, unpathetic, direct, employing only a minimum of mimic devices'.[3] But several reviewers also make equally clear that her technique of 'underplaying' the role, far from precluding emotion or preventing the illusion that the character was 'real', actually enhanced the persuasive power of her interpretation, as in this remark: 'Weigel's Courage was felt to be deeply moving in her moments of pain.'[4] Another critic summed up his experience thus: 'At last a great actress showed once more that perfect, un-learnable correspondence between word and mimic expression, between sound and gesture, between a way of walking and a way of looking. One simply has to dig out that very hackneyed epithet "inspired" to say anything more about the experience.'[5] This impression was shared by Brecht's old friend from Augsburg days, Otto Müllereisert, who wrote, 'the spectator shares the heroine's joy and pain during the action as if they were his own and feels a close bond between the character and himself.'[6]

Such responses were the rule rather than the exception. They confirm, as a fact of theatrical life, that spectators readily adapt to whatever acting or presentational conventions are employed. Willingly suspending their disbelief, they then concentrate on the human content of the performance. If one considers the imaginative capacity of children to enter the world of Punch and Judy, it is hardly surprising that Weigel's fundamentally realistic acting (she spoke the part with a dialect colouring) had a powerfully illusionistic effect, with the result that most critics commented on the persuasiveness and emotional impact of the central characters, and not, as Friedrich Luft did, on the actors' maintenance of critical distance between themselves and the part they were playing.

In theory Brecht did not want the mimetic persuasiveness of any performance to be so powerful as to make the spectator feel that the actor 'was' the character rather than its presenter. Yet this is precisely how Weigel's Courage affected the writer Anna Seghers. Brecht himself, far from regarding it as an 'annihilating verdict' on her acting, was quite clearly proud to be able to note in his journal that mothers watching a procession pointed out Weigel to their children, saying, 'Look, there is Mother Courage'. (Aj, 924)

Despite his theoretical opposition to the organic conception of dramatic character, Brecht in fact built up any given role as an individual with a particular set of qualities – albeit contradictory ones – who is seen to develop from experience to experience. When, for example, he makes Courage refuse to allow her expensive shirts to be torn up for bandages, he argues that her increased hardness is motivated by her loss of Swiss Cheese. Particularly when working in the realistic mode of a play like *Courage*, it seems that Brecht's work was informed less by abstract

Bertolt Brecht

preconceptions than by the *Bretterinstinkt* (theatrical instinct) which, as a young man, he took to be the pre-
requisite for creating convincing theatre in any given mode.

Courage's refusal to hand over the officers' shirts
voluntarily is one of a number of changes introduced by
Brecht in the hope of eliciting a more critical response to
the heroine than that evinced by those commentators on
Leopold Lindtberg's Zürich production of 1943, who had
been struck more by the 'universal mother' aspect of the
figure and by the fated, unfree quality of her 'animal-like',
instinctively led life, than by her sociological significance as
an embodiment of entrepreneurial self-interest. Although
the version of the text played in Zürich already contained
many of the details which, in Brecht's view, argued for a
critical appraisal of Courage's conduct, he decided to
increase the elements on the negative side of the balance
for the Berlin production. However, there is no reason to
suppose that the intended effect was the one actually
achieved. Seen in relation to the loss of Swiss Cheese and
the constant struggle to make a living, Courage's refusal to
hand over the shirts for bandages makes her a more
credible figure than in the earlier version. And it is
precisely because the increased plausibility arises from
seeing her as a person moulded – or deformed – by
objective social circumstance, that the change does not
oblige the spectator to take a simply condemnatory view of
her behaviour.

Related to this question of the limiting or conditioning
influence on behaviour of social and material factors, there
is a further problem concerning the relation of theory to
practice in Brecht's theatre. In order to intuit the reasons
for Mother Courage's refusal to hand out the shirts it is
necessary for the spectator to enter her situation by an act
of identification or empathy – the very Aristotelian form of

108

response to theatrical events against which Brecht directed so much venom. Nor is this an isolated exception to an otherwise firmly established principle in his theatrical practice. On the contrary, his directing, with its entirely conventional reliance on the suggestive power of this gesture or that expression consistently exploits the empathetic ability of the audience (which in any case is the necessary condition of communication within the, broadly speaking, realistic theatrical tradition of the West, lacking as it does the elaborately and explicitly codified set of symbolic conventions on which much oriental theatre is based).

Rather than think of Brecht's work as dispensing with the spectator's empathy, it is better to think of it as an attempt to manipulate the identificatory process and to steer it in particular directions. Thus the scene where Mother Courage is shown, triumphantly singing, immediately (in theatrical time) after she has cursed the war, presupposes the working of empathy at a number of levels. Empathy in the technical sense is involved in interpreting Mother Courage's expressions of feelings, just as intuition is required to relate these feelings to her present material success. The shock-effect of the scene depends, further, on the spectator's having identified – in the sense of sympath-ised – with Courage in the previous scene. Nor does this identification with Courage simply cease when, with the bandaged Kattrin by her side, she marches along singing the praise of war and trading. Her admittedly only too evident faults do nothing to make her less affecting as a human being, for how many spectators could honestly deny ever having been blinded by a sense of immediate personal well-being to the cost of that well-being to others, or could pretend never to have had profound experiences or insights that later faded? The educative shock-effect of the scene thus depends on the spectator's continuing, disturbing, identification with Mother Courage, and simultaneously with the point of view of those pulling the wagon while she walks freely. In other words, empathy, in a variety of forms, was a central element in Brecht's strategy of using the theatre to provoke insight and, as he hoped, action based on that insight.

Those spectators who felt intensely affected by Weigel's realistic playing of Courage, or by Angelika Hurwicz's presentation of Kattrin's complex mix of feelings as she desperately tries to drum the citizens of Halle awake, were not responding in an aberrant manner nor to aberrant realisations of Brecht's intentions. They were responding to the convincing sense of life (for want of a better term) that informed the play and the production. This powerful illusion that the characters and incidents were taken from life permitted Brecht unusual latitude in deploying various forms of stylisation, both in the writing and in the production of his plays, in order to urge a particular view of events on the spectator. On a verbal level, he peppered the dialogue with unusual, witty formulations that etch themselves in the memory. For example, he would produce surprise effects by using a noun with a verb that is usually used with its antonym: 'Don't tell me peace has broken out, just after I laid in new stock' (5ii, 61). The army chaplain uses slang when talking about the most solemn subject, Christ's passion: 'Cases of people getting clobbered like this are by no means unknown in the history of religion' (5ii, 36; adapted).

On a visual level the general plausibility of the central figures and their dilemmas permitted Brecht to underline his social or moral satire by physical or behavioural caricature: the captain who exploits Eilif's 'boldness' is a drunken sot whose praise for the 'pious warrior' carries a suggestion of homosexuality. When the initially attractive whore, Yvette, achieves social advancement, the ugliness of her body and manner emphasise the price she has paid for success, as does the figure of the doddering, impotent Colonel, whose mistress she now is. In Berlin both the cook and the chaplain were played as 'caricatures after the manner of Callot'.[6]

However, such stylisation remained peripheral to the overall effect of (tragic) realism produced by the play. Whereas most playwrights would have been delighted to make such an impact, to have gone so far down the road of realism created problems for Brecht. His ideal was 'combative realism', that is to produce convincing images of life that would nevertheless give rise to specific, predictable responses from the spectator. But the two elements in this conception proved very difficult to marry. Whenever he attempted to retain tight control over character and situation, through strong stylisation or by moving in the direction of allegory, the indefinable feel of life tended to suffer (this difficulty arose particularly with *The Good Person of Szechwan*). On the other hand when, as in *Mother Courage*, he gave freer rein to his natural feel for life, the realism of the figures provoked a variety of interpretations and evaluations much as life itself does.

Even after Brecht had changed the text, had shared the direction of the first Berlin production, and had put Helene Weigel in the leading role, he found that many commentators still did not get the intended 'message', but interpreted it in more or less the same ways as those who had seen Therese Giehse playing Courage in Zürich under Lindtberg's direction. Some saw in the Brecht production a hymn to the common man (or woman), indestructable despite all that history could throw at him. Others saw in it a pessimistic picture of man's inherent weakness and proneness to evil. A (communist) variant of this response was to attack the play for its decadence and defeatism. While one commentator declared that it was not a propagandist contribution to the class struggle, another acknowledged that the playwright's intention was didactic, but claimed that the audience was likely to ignore this and simply relish the richness of his characters.

There is no need to assume obtuseness or malevolence on the part of the commentators to account for such evaluations of the play. They are explicable, rather, as responses to features of the text and its performance which made it very difficult for Brecht to achieve the effects he declaredly intended. One source of difficulty is the complex conception of Mother Courage's situation. Mother Courage is not simply a nasty businesswoman who also happens to have some children. Nor is she simply a good mother gone to the bad because of personal failings. She is an energetic, capable human being who, in the attempt to provide for her family and herself by following the rules of survival current in her society, experiences the conflict inherent in that society between human productivity on the one hand, and the social exploitation of productivity on the other. The destruction of Courage and her family by these deep-seated contradictions in class-society reveals more than she can possibly comprehend. It is difficult even for the reader – and more so for the theatrical spectator – to hold a steady focus on Courage, for she embodies *all* the features observed by critics: she is an example of the ordinary man's will and capacity to survive, a destructive and self-destructive obsessive, a cynical collaborator and a deeply-suffering, well-intentioned victim of the machinations of the powerful. Because she is all of these things, it requires what Brecht himself aptly defined as the difficult

art of 'complex seeing' to grasp the complementary relations between the contradictory facets of her conduct.

A further source of difficulty for Brecht's didactic
enterprise is his use of allusion, usually with the intention of
underlining the peculiarity of what his play shows by calling
to mind a familiar model that both resembles and contrasts
with some aspect of the play. Thus, the chaplain sings the
'Song of the Hours', concerning Christ's Passion, during
the scene in which Swiss Cheese is executed. By analogy,
this puts Mother Courage in the situation of the Mother of
Sorrows. But, as she then has to deny that Swiss Cheese is
her son in order to save her own skin, she is also put in the
situation of Peter denying Christ (a motif that appears
repeatedly, obsessively even, throughout Brecht's
oeuvre). As her business dealings are partly responsible for
Swiss Cheese's death – her bitter reward for betraying him
is the chain of silver coins she earns with the sale of the
wagon – she is also in the situation of Judas. I take it that the
intention of these allusions is to 'de-mythologize' the
Biblical story, by re-interpreting the relation of model and
reality. Whereas Christ's Passion and the roles in it of Judas
and Mary are commonly taken to express a general,
symbolic truth about the 'eternal' martyrdom and suffering
of goodness in a world corrupted by evil, Brecht's
concretisation of the model was presumably intended to be
read as saying that the recurrence throughout history of the
martyrdom of the 'Son of Man' arises from man's own
failure to construct a form of society in which men would be
free of the material pressures that produce their guilt and
their suffering: at bottom, suffering is all a matter of the
production and distribution of wealth.

However, although the relation of event to model can be
understood like this, the reverse is more likely to be the
case, particularly because of the relative power exercised

by words and visual, physical images in stage performance. What the spectator sees, and inevitably identifies with, is a mother's suffering, culminating in Weigel's famous silent scream. This sense of suffering is intensified, rather than undermined, by the spectator's simultaneous awareness of her guilt (of which, as he knows, she is also aware), and by seeing her forced to perform the charade of denying their kinship.

The effect of this scene is multiplied throughout the play. Although full of historical inaccuracies and anachronisms, *Mother Courage* conjures up the seventeenth century setting of the action by numerous allusions to the religious and literary concerns of the baroque period. In the self-understanding of the times, the religious war had made Christ's martyrdom a contemporary reality, giving renewed life to the *topoi* of the transience of earthly existence, the vanity of man's efforts to control life, the fickleness of Fortuna (whose rolling ball or wheel is hinted at in the rise and fall of Courage's business, and possibly even in the turning of the stage and of the wheels on her wagon).

If Brecht's hope was to make the audience relate this baroque ideology to the historically specific base of early capitalist society, he was taking a very dangerous gamble, particularly in presenting the play to an audience that had just lived through the Second World War. Heinrich Kilger's 'Crown of Thorns' design of the lettering in the names of the various locations, the heavily emphasised circularity of Courage's career (the play opens with the wagon being pulled onto and around an empty stage, and closes with it being pulled around and off an empty stage), the seasonal progression from the beginning of spring to the depths of winter, the transformation of Courage from a cheerful, energetic woman in her middle years into a broken, bent and desperate old woman, the dramatic rhythm whereby the frequency and intensity of scenes of suffering increase as the 'epic' chronicle unfolds; the cumulative effect of all this was virtually bound to ensure that the play was received and remembered above all as a tragedy of the suffering of ordinary people across the centuries, while the indictment of petit-bourgeois collaboration could not be expected to play more than a subsidiary role. *If* this is to be accounted a failure, measured against Brecht's didactic intentions, it is surely of less importance than the undoubted achievement of Brecht, the theatrical practitioner, in keeping his audience's attention concentrated on a complex and painful subject.

7
The Life of Galileo

As a subject of literature, the life of Galileo Galilei, the physicist, astronomer and mathematician, who was required by the Inquisition in 1633 to recant his heretical arguments in support of the Copernican opinion that the earth revolved around the sun, would seem to lend itself equally well to heroic or tragic treatment. In popular memory he is celebrated as an embodiment of heroic stubbornness who supposedly bent to the superior power of the Holy See only to retract his recantation at the earliest opportunity with the famous words, '*Eppur si muove*' ('Yet it does move'). On the other hand there is congenial material for the tragedian in the humiliation of the great man at the hands of a church to which he remained deeply attached, in Galileo's isolation, loss of freedom and the growing sadness of his last years. In the successive versions of Brecht's play on this subject there is a shift in emphasis away from a heroic treatment of an individual life towards one in which the individual provides the focus for a study of the historical process, a process that cannot be confined within the limits of pessimistic or optimistic literary modes. The intellectual and emotional complexity of Brecht's final version can best be appreciated by considering the stages by which he arrived at it.

Brecht's first sketches for the play, dating from 1938, indicate that it was intended to relate directly to the struggle against fascism. Here Galileo is the type of 'progressive' intellectual whose interests include the solution of practical problems, who is committed to the cause of free thought and argument on the basis of observed fact, and is therefore opposed to the dogmatism and submission to traditional authority still prevalent in the intellectual establishment of the day—the Catholic Church. Most importantly, Galileo understands the *political* function of religious dogma as the ideological prop of the ruling interests in feudal society, and is conscious of the fact that his challenge to the authority of the Church in the intellectual field places him on the side of those whose vital interests would be served by technological, economic and social change.

One of Brecht's early working notes reads: 'Beginning of the play. Three cardinals discuss Galileo's discoveries and the need to do something against them. More or less in the same manner as three executives of a chemical concern would use to talk about a researcher who posed a threat to their monopolies.'[1] When the Inquisition then threatens him with torture Galileo recants, it is true, but this apparent acceptance of defeat is in fact a stratagem that permits Galileo to survive and continue his researches. These, when smuggled out to the 'free' world, will reveal the Church's inability to stifle man's urge to know. In his political conduct, as in his methods of empirical research, Galileo demonstrates the power of the dialectical principle formulated by his near contemporary, Francis Bacon: '*Non*

117

nisi pariendo natura vincitur' – 'Only by submitting to it can nature be conquered.' This first interpretation of Galileo's life was clearly inspired by the wish to give a message of hope in dark times, and thereby to encourage the view that resistance to unreasoning tyranny (represented in the present by fascism) was both possible and indeed assured of eventual success because history, which had vindicated Galileo, was inherently on the side of reason and social progress.

By the time Brecht had completed the first, so-called 'Danish' version of the play, however, the conception of the scientist as an underground resistance worker had already been modified to allow for an element of personal weakness in the conduct of the hero. In the penultimate scene, where Galileo has his last, all-important conversation with his former pupil, Andrea, Galileo's recantation is no longer presented as a well-considered tactical withdrawal; rather, he confesses, it was prompted by sheer fear of pain. More importantly, Galileo's public recantation, in his own assessment, was not simply a denial of particular scientific truths but represented the dereliction of his more general duty to fight for the right to pursue and publish the truth, wherever it might lead, and in all areas of human inquiry. As a result of this wider betrayal, Galileo concludes, he no longer deserves to be considered a member of the community of science.

The circumstances in which Galileo pronounces this self-condemnation are such that one cannot be sure how seriously he intends it to be taken. Up to the point when he declares that he is an outcast from the realm of science the whole interview with Andrea has been conducted in the presence of his pious daughter Virginia who is in agreement with the Church's opposition to her father's scientific work. In fact it is the vehemence with which he castigates himself in front of Andrea that persuades Virginia that there is no need for her to continue supervising the conversation, and she leaves with the passionate words, 'But you have been admitted into the ranks of the faithful!' (GM, 37) Left alone with Andrea, however, Galileo's tone changes as he confesses that he has not been completely free of 'relapses' into his old scientific habits. The 'weakness of his flesh' which he previously blamed for his submission to the power of the Inquisition now becomes something positive, for it has led him to complete the 'Discorsi', in which he has furnished the arguments needed to vindicate Copernicus's theory of the universe.

Although, aware that they may yet be overheard, Galileo still describes his continued scientific work in negative terms – 'I keep succumbing to temptation. I shouldn't work but I do. I am the slave of my habits, and my punishment will be hard one day.' (GM, 38) It is clear that he has risked great danger and destroyed his eyesight in order to advance the cause of science. Before Andrea departs with the 'Discorsi' under his jacket Galileo considerably revises his assessment of his 'betrayal' of science:

I am glad to find you as you are. Certain experiences might have led you to a quite wrong view about what we always referred to as the future of reason. But of course a single individual can neither lend reason authority nor bring it into discredit. It is too great a thing for that. Reason is something that men have in common. In fact it is the selfishness of the whole of humanity. This selfishness is too weak, but even a man like me can see that reason is not finished but is just beginning. I still hold to the view that this is a new age. Even if it might look like a blood-smeared old whore, that's just the way a new age

would look! Light breaks into the very depths of
darkness.

(GM, 20)

Despite his guilt at his failure to profess his faith in
science publicly, Galileo's life is largely redeemed by his
works. Science and the cause of humanity have wrested
from him what they needed – the 'Discorsi' – even if the
cost was the destruction of his self-esteem and his health.
On balance, then, this version of the play still offered in the
end a positive view of history progressing unstoppably, if
erratically, despite the failings of individuals. Interestingly
enough, this is the version currently in the repertoire of the
Berliner Ensemble.

The 'American' version of *Galileo*, now the most widely
used text of the play, came about as a result of further
revisions which Brecht felt compelled to make in the light
of experiences that had seriously undermined the assumptions about historical progress with which he had first
embarked on the project. In 1945 Brecht was working in
California with Charles Laughton on a translation of the
play into English for a production in which Laughton was to
take the leading role, when the news broke that America
had dropped the Atom Bomb on Hiroshima. 'Overnight',
Brecht recalled, 'the biography of the founder of modern
physics read quite differently.' (GM, 55) Galileo's dedication to the 'pure' truth of science, of which Brecht had
originally approved, had allowed the products of science to
become instruments in the very impure hands of politi-
cians. Galileo's recantation now appeared to Brecht to
represent the 'original sin' of science. His biography
therefore had to be transformed from a model of covert
resistance to oppression into a negative example of the
amoral, apolitical intellectual who fails to consider, first

and foremost, the social context and consequences of his work. Brecht now wanted to make it clear that Galileo's scientific achievements in no way justified his public betrayal of the integrity of scientific truth. However, the actual effect of the textual revisions that were designed to cast an unsparingly critical light on a figure who had originally been seen positively, was to create a complex, contradictory and ambiguous whole that permits neither simple admiration nor simple condemnation of Galileo.

In re-casting the life of Galileo, Brecht had in mind not just the 'criminal' irresponsibility of the nuclear physicists who collaborated on the development of the atom bomb but also broader considerations of the nature and social role of the intellectual. Although set in seventeenth-century Italy, the play has obvious relevance to the question of '*die deutsche Misere*', that is, Marx's critique of the traditional failure of German intellectuals, particularly in the bourgeois era, to put their gifts at the service of the revolutionary social movements of their times. There are in the play overtones of Luther's challenge to the authority of the Papacy, and of his translation of the Bible into the vernacular, but also of his siding with the princes in their oppression of the peasants. There are hints, too, of developments that issued in later, decadent forms of bourgeois thought, of Nietzsche's 'joyful science', of his proclamation that 'God is dead', of his 'laughing' Zarathustra and the concomitant scorn for all 'lesser' beings.

Yet there are also parallels between the problems of the emerging bourgeois epoch in seventeenth-century Italy and those of the new age of the proletariat in the twentieth century: just as Galileo's pursuit of scientific truth was hindered not only by a 'reactionary' church but also by the tight-fistedness and short-sightedness of the 'progressive' bourgeois authorities in Venice, so the free development of socialist thought in the present was threatened not only by the dark irrationalism of fascism but also by the Stalinisation of the Russian Revolution, by the Moscow Trials and by the Hitler–Stalin Pact (made after the first version of *Galileo*). In fact Brecht's contradictory evaluation of Stalin's historical role provides a useful pointer to the view of history underlying the standard version of *The Life of Galileo*.

In correspondence with his Marxist mentor, Karl Korsch, who had come to believe that the Russian Revolution had been betrayed by Stalin, Brecht argued for a dialectical-materialist interpretation of events in Russia since the Revolution.[2] As he interpreted it, the revolution of 1917 was in essence a setting free of enormous productive forces that the previous socio-economic system had failed to develop. The subsequent progress of the Revolution therefore had to be understood as a process whereby those productive energies sought the conditions necessary for their own development. In this view Stalin's dictatorship was the form of rule necessitated by the continuing struggle of the proletariat against the forces of Reaction threatening the new society from without and within. Stalinism was thus not simply the product of one individual's character, but had resulted rather from an interaction between the urgent need to develop rapidly the forces of production in Russia and objective historical constraints. Yet, despite the arguments from historical necessity he put to Korsch, Brecht privately took a critical view both of the politics and the morality of Stalin. A similar conflict between materialist-determinist philosophy and the application of ethical standards to the individual permeates the view of history presented by *The Life of Galileo*.

The opening scene shows Galileo at the beginning of a

day in 1609 when he was a teacher of mathematics at the university of Padua in the merchant republic of Venice. He is a vigorous man in middle age (he is forty-six) whose lust for life is evident in the way he washes himself, breakfasts and at the same time gives an impromptu lesson in mathematics and cosmology to the boy Andrea, son of his housekeeper, Signora Sarti. His pleasure in the physical, intellectual and social aspects of life is supported by the enthusiastic belief that he is living in a 'new age'. By the end of the play, some thirty years later, the unity has disappeared from Galileo's life. He has become a greedy old man, boorish, cynical and bitter, whose still sharp intellect dissects mercilessly his own faults and those of others, although he has not entirely lost the conviction that a new age has begun. He has completed the 'Discorsi' and is pleased that Andrea will smuggle them out into the hands of other scientists, but no sooner has he put the manuscript into Andrea's hands than he launches, with malicious pleasure, into a diatribe implicating his pupil in his own crime of putting scientific values above all others. Read retrospectively, through the eyes of the embittered Galileo, this life has been one of abject moral failure. Brecht, too, judged it in this way on occasion, and hoped to make his audience share this view. However, as Brecht himself remarked in relation to the Danish version of the play, Epic Theatre does not accord greater emphasis to the ending of a play than it does to the preceding scenes. (GM, 50) Read sequentially, Galileo's life reveals history to be a process in which the individual is so subject to the awesome combined effects of nature and circumstance, that it is not easy to subject a life to moral judgement.

The causes that will eventually destroy the unity of Galileo's personality are already present, although not yet readily apparent as such, in the opening scene. They are to be found both in his personality and in his society, or to be more precise, in the interaction of these two things. Galileo's personality clearly bears the stamp of his times. His is an age of discovery, expansion, innovation and adventure that inspires – or seduces – Galileo to share in the pleasure of extending man's mastery over the world of nature. On the other hand, Galileo's view of his age is subjectively coloured by his own energetic, imaginative, expansive nature. It is *his* sense of being on the brink of important scientific advances, *his* enthusiasm for movement rather than stasis, for doubt and enquiry rather than belief, for freedom and openness rather than for restriction and enclosure, that makes him proclaim to Andrea, 'the old age is past and a new age is here'. It is the excitement of the astronomer about a new 'emancipated' cosmology in which the universe has lost its fixed centre, 'so that each – and none – is regarded as its centre', that leads him to make generalisations about impending changes in the world of men, generalisations which fail to take adequate account of the resistance that will be offered by the hierarchical order of feudal society to anything that threatens its stability. Of course, Galileo 'knows' that not everyone will share his enthusiasm for new ideas – he warns Andrea not to broadcast what he has told him – but he does not let this knowledge govern his behaviour. It is appropriate that Galileo is first shown in conversation with the boy Andrea, for his own personality has a markedly naive, boyish streak. He is, in every sense, a 'child of the new age', and is treated as such by Andrea's mother, Signora Sarti.

Signora Sarti is the first of a series of characters introduced in the first scene to provide a contrast between Galileo's paean to the new age and the social and political realities of the times. She scolds him for teaching Andrea things that would cause trouble with the authorities if the boy were to repeat them in school, and she insists that he take on a rich private pupil so that the milk can be paid for. In later scenes Signora Sarti remains personally loyal to Galileo, even to the point of exposing herself to the plague in order to look after him, but she remains adamant that his ideas are 'of the devil' and encourages his daughter, Virginia, to consult a 'real' astronomer (an astrologist!) about her forthcoming marriage; the implication is that such superstition is more typical of the attitudes of ordinary people than Galileo's enthusiasm for scientific demonstration and innovation.

The new paying pupil, Ludovico Marsili, represents the opposite end of the social scale, the rich and powerful landed aristocracy. On the one hand, the fact that he has been sent by his mother to learn some science from Galileo indicates that the regard for science is rising and spreading in Italian society, but on the other hand it is equally apparent that the interest of the Marsilis is dilettante ('Nobody can drink a glass of wine without science these days you know' – 5i, 13) and will *not* extend to a welcome for the socially emancipatory implications Galileo sees in his researches.

A third section of society is then introduced in the person of the curator of Padua university, who brings the bad news that Galileo's employers are unwilling to grant him the increase in salary that would relieve him of the necessity of wasting time on teaching private pupils when it could more fruitfully be devoted to the pursuit of original research. Even the most progressive social force in contemporary Italy, the burghers of the Republic of Venice, have at best a limited interest in Galileo's new science. They are willing to pay 'scudi' only for what earns them scudi, financing science only insofar as it promises them immediate practical rewards in the mercantile or military spheres.

Put in Marxist terms, the opening scene shows that there is at work in Galileo a productive *force* (in this case an intellectual one) far greater than can be contained within the particular, limited *forms* of production presently available in society, including those being developed by the bourgeoisie. Put in personal terms, the novelty of Galileo's way of looking at and thinking about the world makes him unable to see things in the same perspective as the majority of his contemporaries. This double conflict shapes the ensuing action.

Resenting the attitude of the Venetian authorities who, because they permit freedom of research, feel free to pay low salaries to their scholars, Galileo seeks feudal patronage in Florence, where he hopes that the young Duke Cosmo de Medici will support his work in exchange for the honour of having a constellation of stars, newly discovered with the aid of the telescope, named after him. Galileo is granted patronage but the young Duke is still under the control of older courtiers, among them traditional scholars who, threatened by the rise of a new, empirical science, refuse to test the authority of Aristotle against the evidence of their own eyes. As predicted by Galileo's friends in Padua, opposition to his ideas in Florence leads to his work being referred to the Papal astronomer in Rome, Pater Clavius. When Clavius, to the consternation of the clerical establishment, confirms Galileo's findings, Galileo exclaims, '*It* has won. Not me: reason has won.' (5i, 54) However, his sense of victory is premature, for the Inquisition immediately puts the Copernican theory on the Index of forbidden teachings; the fact that is true speaks *against* rather than for the theory in the view of those whose prime concern is the defence of the authority, power and vested interests of the Catholic Church. Although angry, and aware that to preserve silence on the matter is to allow the Church to preserve a show of infallibility that is part and parcel of its maintenance of a hierarchical and exploitative social system, Galileo submits to the prohibition. Yet, because his urge to advance the science of astronomy is too strong to be suppressed, he secretly continues his observations throughout eight years of silence.

As soon as he hears that Cardinal Barberini, a man with a scientific training, has been elected Pope, Galileo believes he will again be free to publish his findings. Once again his faith in reason is proved to be misplaced, for the new Pope, despite personal scruples, yields to the view of the Inquisitor that Galileo's defiance of the Church's authority is intolerable, particularly now that the dispute has become common knowledge and the common people are threatening to turn that knowledge against the established order of things. When shown the instruments of torture, Galileo agrees to recant publicly his belief in the correctness of Copernican theory. For the remainder of his life Galileo is kept under house arrest. He is provided with every comfort, including pen and paper. What he writes, however, is taken away by his gaolers.

Yet Galileo's submission to the authority of the Church, even to the extent of endorsing the suppression of a popular uprising, is less complete than it seems, for, driven by an unabated impulse to define and publish the truth about the physical world, he secretly writes a copy of the 'Discorsi' by moonlight, thereby destroying his already damaged powers of sight. Thus, in the end he is able to frustrate the attempts of the Church to curtail the development of knowledge, but this victory is tainted by a profound sense of guilt at having been too cowardly to challenge the Church publicly in 1633, when such a challenge could have had enormous political consequences. As it is, his silence enabled the forces of reaction to retrench, so that now even the publication of the 'Discorsi' must remain an event with relatively slight political repercussions. Galileo has failed to take the tide of history at the flood.

Brecht did not want *The Life of Galileo* to be regarded as an individual tragedy. One of the changes in the 'American' version was the arrival of the iron-founder, Vanni, at a crucial juncture to warn Galileo of his impending summons by the Inquisition, to offer him a means of escape, and to assure him of the support of the manufacturing classes, particularly in the Northern cities of Italy. Had Galileo accepted this offer of help, Brecht argued, he could have avoided arraignment before the Inquisition and hence the damaging personal and social consequences of his recantation.

Yet the sense of tragedy could not be eliminated from the play simply by the insertion of this brief exchange with Vanni. This example of Brecht's use of the 'not . . . but' technique was intended to make the audience aware that Galileo did not make this choice but rather the one that leads to the catastrophe. But the alternative, non-catastrophic outcome would only have been a real possibility had Galileo's character been different. Galileo refuses Vanni's offer for what seem to him to be good reasons. Partly it is because he does not believe the merchant classes have the power to protect him from the Inquisition: 'I can distinguish power from impotence' (5i, 88). He has not forgotten the fate of Giordano Bruno who was handed over to the Inquisition *by the Venetian authorities* just thirty years previously to be burned for the self-same 'heresy' of arguing that the earth was not the centre of the world. Galileo prefers to rely on the protection of his powerful patron, the Duke of Florence, and on the fact that the Pope is a trained scientist. His judgement is proved wrong by subsequent events, but the audience is not given sufficient evidence about the political situation to recognise in advance why Galileo's choice is the wrong one.

However, even if Brecht had filled in the political background more fully (as one might have expected in Epic Theatre), so as to demonstrate not only that the challenge of the middle classes to the feudal order had become very strong, but also that Galileo's defiance of the Church's intellectual authority was crucial to that challenge, Galileo's refusal of Vanni's help would nevertheless have remained more plausible than the opposite. Despite his sympathy for the oppressed and his respect for the artisans, Galileo has been shown from the outset to possess little political sensitivity. As Brecht said, he simply does not know how to take a hint. He is also inclined to stay in Florence because he enjoys physical comfort and because, being an exceptional man himself, he naively believes in exceptions: the Duke is bound to protect him, or at least the scientist-Pope will. Galileo's fatal errors, in other words, are deeply rooted in his character.

Contrary to Brecht's express intentions, *The Life of Galileo* produces the effects of tragedy. It even conforms in a number of respects to Aristotle's account of the genre. As the story of a great man's fall its subject has the magnitude appropriate to the genre. Moreover, his fall is brought about by the same qualities that make him great (tragic irony), and these qualities are deeply rooted in his personal disposition (tragic necessity). In making him an unusually sensuous man who thinks productively because of the *pleasure* thinking affords him, nature simultaneously made him a man incapable of withstanding the *pain* of torture. Being gifted with a new way of seeing, Galileo is unable, in consequence, to perceive things that are very plain to others less gifted than himself but more attuned to the ways of existing society. The very faults which Brecht stressed in order to set this life at a critical distance from the audience make of him the type of 'mixed character' traditionally thought necessary for tragedy to secure the belief and sympathy of the audience. Galileo's fateful choices are further constrained by the objective social conditions of his times: he only moved to aristocratic Florence because republican Venice did not offer him the working conditions he needed.

Not only does *Galileo* stand up to analysis in terms of Aristotelian *hamartia* (tragic error or flaw), the play also, even more surprisingly, has an obvious affinity with Nietzsche's 'Dionysian account of tragedy; that is, one which sees in the tragic hero the embodiment of an energy so great that it destroys its bearer. The parallel is suggested by Galileo's words: 'And the worst thing is that what I know I must tell people. Like a lover, like a drunkard, like a traitor.' (5i, 68) A laconic observation of Brecht's suggests the same connection: 'His productiveness destroys him.' (GM, 37) As Brecht understood it (whether the audience would see it in the same way is another question), Galileo's *Forschungstrieb* or scientific impulse, the specific form of his productive energy, was a 'social phenomenon', as much motivated by the desire to communicate knowledge as to create it. Even allowing for this, however, the argument of the play remains tragic, a Marxist variation on a Nietzschean theme: Galileo's tragedy was to be born into an age that stimulated more productivity in him than the society of the time would or could accommodate.

The tragic interplay of character and circumstance in *The Life of Galileo* raises the question whether Brecht failed here in his project to create a practicable type of theatre, one that would enable the audience to master life's problems, rather than one which discouraged hopeful action by dwelling on unavoidable and unmanageable problems. I would argue that the opposition between tragic and epic theatre, for which Brecht himself was largely responsible, fails to do justice to the achievement of a play like *Galileo*. The play certainly shows the destructive consequences, both for himself and for others, of Galileo's peculiar combination of giftedness and weakness. On the other hand, the play also shows the urge to know and spread the truth asserting itself despite persecution and even in spite of the individual's own fear of this inner compulsion. Having heard Galileo's bitter self-analysis (which in any case smacks too much of *Brecht's* hindsight), Andrea refuses to believe that such a harsh verdict will be the last word on the question of Galileo's achievements. The audience, although as much aware of the pupil Andrea's partiality as of Galileo's, is likely to agree with him.

Perhaps more important, however, is the fact that the play shows Galileo's tragedy in its connection with the specific socio-economic conditions of the epoch in which it occurred. The practicable aspect of this approach lies in its demonstration of what is the destructive *rule*, rather than the fortunate exception, in antagonistic class-society. The tragic aspect of the play is bound up with its radicalism: to avoid this kind of tragedy, society needs to organise itself in such a way that the productive potential of the individual is not forced or tempted to take on anti-social forms.

Galileo is probably the most intellectual and discursive of Brecht's plays. Nevertheless it can be very effective in performance, largely because Brecht's eminently theatrical imagination knew how to exploit the varied resources of the stage to hold the attention of the audience. Although there exists no record of a complete production for which Brecht was responsible (Joseph Losey directed the American production, and Brecht died during rehearsals for the production at the Berliner Ensemble), his notes, particularly those of his collaboration with Charles Laughton, indicate how he thought the play should be staged.

Brecht's aim was to make Galileo's biography the focus of a study in social history. One of the means by which he sought to draw attention to the social significance of the *Fabel* was costume. Costume figures most prominently in the scene where the Pope (previously Cardinal Barberini) is urged by the Inquisitor to silence Galileo. The scene opens dramatically with his outright refusal (*'very loudly*: "No! No! No!"'), but ends with the concession that 'at the most' Galileo should be shown the instruments of torture; the Inquisitor, who knows his victim, is fully satisfied. As they discuss the matter, two other things are happening on and off-stage: Barberini is being dressed in full papal vestments, while from outside the chamber there comes the sound of many people walking up and down as they await an audience with the Pope. What this makes clear is that the decision to put pressure on Galileo is taken, not by Barberini, an individual with a scientific training, but by Urban VIII, the bearer of an office which requires that he put the interests of the Church above all personal considerations. Once he is in full papal robes he can no longer deny the Inquisitor the consent he demands.

This dressing-scene recalls, by way of contrast, the opening scene of the play where Galileo, who first appears stripped to the waist, dresses and breakfasts in the company of Andrea before receiving visits from better situated members of society. Galileo's initial nakedness reveals the plentiful, and soft, flesh that will seek out the 'fleshpots' of Venice and shrink from the Inquisitor's instruments of torture. It also represents the 'naked humanity' or naiveté underlying his repeated misjudgements of the political situation. This theme of symbolic 'nakedness' is then taken up and varied in the Masked Ball scene where Galileo, who wears no mask, is informed by the Cardinals Bellarmin and Barberini (bearing the masks of a lamb and a dove!), that the Copernican doctrine has been proscribed. As well as creating clear patterns that can be apprehended intellectually, these contrasts of the naked and the clothed, when seen on stage, have a strong tactile-emotive effect that is at odds with the playwright's declared intention to create distance between audience and characters.

Brecht created an effective theatrical link between Galileo's professional distinction and his political insensitivity by means of the complementary motifs of seeing and not-seeing. The telescope which enables Galileo to see further into space than his predecessors also symbolises the narrowness of vision associated with his professional enthusiasm. This *déformation professionelle* is brought out early on, in the second scene of the play, when Galileo is so taken up with telling his colleague, Sagredo, about what he has seen through the instrument that he fails to notice offers of congratulation, first from Curator Priuli and then from the Doge of Venice himself. Such incidents recur throughout the play as Galileo's metaphorical blindness is turned into literal blindness by his obsessive and dangerous use of the telescope (to observe sunspots, for example). The motif unfolds its full expressive power in the climactic last conversation between master and pupil where it becomes a focus of contradictory but inter-related associations – with past political misjudgements, with the obsessive, or dedicated, astronomical observation and writing that cost Galileo his eyesight, and with his cunning in persuading his gaolers that his blindness is more complete than it really is. Again, Galileo's blindness is both a source of ironic paradox (he now 'sees' his errors with great clarity) and of pathos.

To help the audience conceptualise such symbolic imagery (of which there is a great deal in the play) Brecht wanted the staging to draw attention to the theatricality of the events being presented: 'The decorations should not be of a kind to suggest to the spectators that they are in a medieval Italian room or the Vatican. The audience should be conscious of being in a theatre.' (5i, 136) The background was to show more than Galileo's immediate surroundings: 'in an imaginative and artistically pleasing way it should show the historical setting' (ibid), for example by reproducing old engravings of Venice or drawings of contemporary fighting ships. This background was to be kept flat so as to enhance the plasticity of the figures. Presumably Brecht would have appreciated the set designed by Luciano Damiani for Giorgio Strehler's Milan production of 1962: 'In a play concerned with science it is appropriate to make the scenic pointers "scientific", that is, studies, architectural sketches in white, black or grey. The human figures are much larger than the architectonic forms that are positioned like signs in the places where they are needed. Thus, for example, the Florentine palace of the Medici becomes a rectangle from an architectural drawing for this palace, is placed on little wheels and pushed on to the stage. In front of it Galileo and his daughter sit on a bench which is larger than normal and wait for the Grand Duke. The relationships are correct.' (GM, 137).

As well as consulting the work of the elder Brueghel for illustrations of the costume of the period, Brecht wanted the grouping of the actors on stage 'to have the quality of historical paintings' (5i, 137), not simply for decorative effect but in order to 'frame' the *Gestus* of any given scene. At the same time both the groupings and the carefully selected, deliberate movements of the actors had to remain quite natural and realistic. In other words, Brecht wanted

134

to create the impression that his carefully constructed 'models' of social history *could* have happened. Despite his assurances to the contrary, he, like most men of the theatre, was in the business of creating illusions. He was not so much pursuing historical truth as working in a historicising mode that would lend plausibility to his ideological constructs. Thus, although the costumes for the American production were *based* on historically verifiable fashions (after considerable, eventually rather desperate, searching), those features which signalled social difference were exaggerated to make these differences clearer to a modern audience.

Whether all this would necessarily have the effect of interesting the audience *principally* in the social and historical questions raised by Galileo's life is another matter. From an early stage Brecht was dissatisfied with the form he had chosen for the play: '*The Life of Galileo* is technically a great step backwards; like *Señora Carrar's Rifles* it is far too opportunistic. The play would have to be completely re-written in order to have that "breeze coming from new coasts", that rosy dawn of science, everything would have to be more direct, without the interiors, the "atmosphere", the empathy, with everything aiming at the effect of a planetary demonstration.' (GM, 35) The 'opportunistic' form had been chosen because Galileo was originally conceived as a positive hero with whom the audience might usefully identify. Since Brecht's subsequent revisions never amounted to the radical re-casting he considered necessary, the play retained its tendency to invite an empathetic response. Brecht then justified this to himself with the thought that the audience, in identifying with Galileo, would at least eventually be led to adopt the 'alienating' view he takes of his own life in the penultimate scene of the play. (Actually this was the *last* scene

performed in both productions in which Brecht was
involved; the last written scene, in which Andrea smuggles
the 'Discorsi' over the Italian border, and the earlier plague
scenes were cut because they threw too positive a light on
Galileo's life.)

Yet the notes on Brecht's work with Laughton and Ernst
Busch, who took the part in Berlin, show that Brecht
himself took intrinsic pleasure both in helping Busch
develop a fascinating psychological portrait and also in
responding empathetically to Laughton's suggestive playing of the role. Brecht's tribute to Laughton's work in the
essay 'Building up a part: Laughton's Galileo' begins with
praise for the way the actor concentrated on the visible,
outward aspects of the scientist's life, on his involvement in
the world around him, and the way Laughton showed 'the
external side not just for the sake of the inner man – that is
to say, research and everything connected with it just for
the sake of the resulting psychological reactions'. (5i, 139)
Yet this generalisation is not entirely borne out by Brecht's
descriptions of particular details of Laughton's performance. Laughton clearly was inventive in devising telling
gestures, but what they revealed was something inward,
the qualities of Galileo's emotional and intellectual life.
These gestures in turn clearly required an empathetic
response from the spectator (in this case Brecht) if their
meaning was to be grasped, as the following comments by
Brecht confirm:

But it was just this mixture of the physical and the
intellectual that attracted L. 'Galileo's physical content-
ment' at having his back rubbed by the boy is transformed into intellectual production. Again, in the ninth
scene, L. brought out the fact that Galileo recovers his
taste for wine on hearing of the reactionary pope's

expected demise. His sensual walking, the play of his hands in his pockets while he is planning new researches, came close to being offensive. Whenever Galileo is creative, L. displayed a mixture of aggressiveness and defenceless softness and vulnerability. (5i, 140–1)

In other words, Laughton's portrayal was rich in the kind of psychological nuance that only communicates itself to the imaginative, sensitive type of spectator who is able to share the perspective of the character. Laughton's acting also elicited a range of emotional responses, as when Galileo was shown to exploit his daughter's loyalty: 'Nonetheless L. succeeded brilliantly in eliciting from the spectator not only a measure of contempt but also a measure of horror at the degradations that debase. And for all this he had only a few sentences and pauses at his disposal'. (5i, 154) The interplay of this kind of emotive subjective matter with a clear intellectual organisation overall is what produces the richness characteristic of Brecht's theatre at its best. This was what Friedrich Luft experienced at Theater am Schiff-bauerdamm in 1957: 'One contemplates the tableau of an exemplary fate, consciously distanced but, precisely because of this, deeply involving and intellectually stimulating.'[3]

8
The Good Person of Szechwan

Brecht began work on this play in 1938, some four months after completing the first version of *The Life of Galileo*. Dissatisfied with the 'opportunism' that had led him to choose the relatively conservative biographical form of the latter play, he launched into the new work, which he cast in the genre of parable, with enthusiasm, aware that there was very little likelihood of it being performed in the near future and, freed of the obligation to write with a particular, immediate purpose, determined to make no 'concessions' to prevailing audience expectations. Having made 'a great step backwards in technique' with *Galileo*, *The Good Person of Sezchwan*, written 'for the bottom drawer' (SM, 13), was to be based much more uncompromisingly on the principles of Epic Theatre.

The genre of parable lent itself to Brecht's conception of 'demonstrational theatre' in a number of ways. The parable, so he explained to Walter Benjamin, was a form of

writing in which the imagination was kept accountable to
reason, the tendency towards autonomy of the aesthetic
impulse being held in check by the obligation to write what
was useful.[1] For Brecht it was a genre that aimed at
transparency: the surface of specific events and characters
served to point beyond (or behind) itself towards general,
'abstract' meanings it illustrated 'concretely'. Because it
does not pretend to be anything other than a made-up
story, clearly told to advance an argument, parable has the
kind of naive relation to reality that Brecht thought was an
important quality of Epic Theatre; the opposite of naiveté
in this sense is naturalism, where the artist seeks to create
the illusion that what his work shows *is* reality.

Although Brecht began writing parables before he
became a Marxist, it was a genre that gained in importance
for him once he had adopted this ideology. This was
because Marxism is concerned not only to establish 'the
laws of social life' (*die Gesetze des menschlichen Zusam-
menlebens*), but also to assert the divergence of what is
'true' from what is 'real'. For the Marxist, the truth about
humanity is not simply a matter of what is observably the
case. This is because he believes that human potentiality
has never been able to find its fullest expression within
historical actuality, because of the fact that men live in an
alienated condition within societies founded on class-
division, competition and exploitation. *The Good Person
of Szechwan* is an example of a parable which illuminates a
'truth' that could never be established by describing life
naturalistically, because the 'good person' in each of us
supposedly disappears at an early age under the pressure of
the alienating conditions of everyday social existence.
Thus, Brecht's *Fabel* invites the audience to consider an
exception in order to make it understand the rule.

In *The Good Person*, what Brecht called the 'element of

parable', the artifice that makes it clear that the play is not pretending simply to mimic life, is constituted by the arrival in the Chinese province of Szechwan of three Gods in search of a good person whose existence will justify the continued existence of the world as it is. The play thus presents itself from the outset as a re-working of an ancient, but very familiar motif, thereby advertising its own literariness and promoting a reflective response from the audience by inviting it to compare the familiar story with the new and, as it turns out, strongly parodistic, version. The search of the Gods serves to lead the audience through a process of learning or enquiry into the question that has driven them from the peaceful 'higher' regions down to earth, the question, namely whether it is possible for a human being both to be good and to survive. In the end, the enquiry becomes a judicial one, the court scene being one of Brecht's favourite devices for recapitulating and explicitly debating the issues raised by the events of a play.

The plot culminating in the trial is itself structured as an argument that implicitly answers the question raised by the Gods. The action proper begins when the water-seller, Wang, asks the obliging Shen Teh to give the newly-arrived Gods shelter for a night. Shen Teh's willingness to help delights – and somewhat surprises – the Gods, for it seems that they have already found in her an example of the goodness they are seeking. However, things are not quite so simple, for it emerges that Shen Teh is a prostitute: although, as her treatment of the Gods shows, she is willing to love her neighbour, she normally has to insist on payment for her love in order to keep herself alive. Somewhat embarrassed by the discovery that she is not the embodiment of untainted virtue they had hoped for, the Gods decide to bend the rules a little by giving her an enormous payment of one thousand silver dollars for the night's accommodation, hoping thereby to enable her to 'sin no more'.

With her dollars Shen Teh makes a fresh start in life by buying a small tobacco shop. However, the reputation for goodness that led to her giving hospitality to the Gods, and hence to her becoming wealthy, threatens to impoverish her almost as quickly, as she is besieged by appeals for charity from the poor of the district. Those she helps perceive more quickly than she does that her resources will soon be exhausted unless she curbs her altruistic impulse 'never to say no'. This conflict between looking after herself and looking after others leads to the introduction of a further clearly parabolic element into the plot, namely the *invention* of a male cousin, Shui Ta, who possesses the toughness in dealing with the spongers that Shen Teh lacks. Ironically, the idea that she should claim to have such a cousin is suggested to Shen Teh by one of those she has helped – in order to drive away others whose claims on her charity would threaten his own enjoyment of it. This sponger is thus not a little surprised when Shui Ta actually appears in the tobacco shop and ruthlessly sorts out the problems Shen Teh has created for herself, which means, among other things, throwing out the 'many-headed family' who, ungrateful as they are, still need to be helped.

What has emerged in Shen Teh's experiences with the poor is confirmed repeatedly in the remainder of the action: that it is impossible, in the world as it is at present, to 'be good and yet to live'. Whenever she attempts to be kind to a group of people or another individual, it quickly emerges that her altruism both threatens her own material interests and involves refusing to help, or even hurting, other people. Reluctantly, but repeatedly, Shen Teh has to 'call in' her make-believe cousin to protect her from the consequences of her kindness. Yet, of course, every time

Shui Ta helps Shen Teh in one sense, 'he' damages her in another, for, in playing the part of the unscrupulous Shui Ta, Shen Teh has to do violence to her own better nature. Even 'winning' in this society means losing. In Shen Teh's world, the parable argues, it is not possible to live as a whole human being with both moral and material needs.

The ambivalence of the Shui Ta stratagem becomes clearer on each of the next two occasions that Shen Teh has to call 'him' in. The first arises after she, an erstwhile prostitute, has allowed herself the luxury of falling in love with just one man. Her lover is Sun, a trained, but unemployed pilot, whom she meets when his despair at not being able to fly has driven him to the point of suicide. In order to help him realise his ambition, Shen Teh has to be prepared to do wrong in a number of ways. What is needed is money to bribe an official who will give Sun a job by taking it away from some other, equally deserving pilot. To raise this sum she resumes the role of her resourceful and ruthless male cousin. Thus disguised, however, she has to endure the painful experience of hearing Sun confide in her that he only wants to marry Shen Teh in order to obtain money to further his career, and has no intention of taking her with him, 'in the first instance', to Peking. Wounded and angry, Shui Ta decides that she must simply give up Sun and solve her own financial problems by marrying the rich, but unattractive barber, Shu Fu. Once she has shed her disguise, however, Shen Teh's heart rules her head once more, and she yields to Sun's insistence that she marry him rather than Shu Fu. Yet this only leads to more pain, for Sun refuses to go through with the wedding when Shui Ta fails to turn up with the expected dowry. Thus, the familiar theatrical device of the male–female disguise makes the moral quite clear: Sun can *either* have the good

142

Shen Teh *or* the wealth provided by Shui Ta, but he cannot have both together.

Shen Teh's next and avowedly 'last' transformation into Shui Ta is precipitated by her discovery that she is pregnant. Having failed to make exceptions of the poor, and then of Sun, she is determined that her son at least will not fall victim to the misery that is the rule of life in Szechwan. This time Shui Ta embarks on a new commercial enterprise, funding it with a cheque for 1,000 dollars offered 'selflessly' to Shen Teh by the amorous barber, Shu Fu. The employees in Shui Ta's sweat-shop are the poor family to whom Shen Teh once gave shelter. The foreman is Sun, his appointment to the position reflecting both Shen Teh's continuing attachment to him and the admixture of bitterness that leads her to implicate him in the brutal and self-damaging practices of Shui Ta. Thus, even the intention of doing good to her own, as yet unborn child, is not compatible with being good to herself, for it too involves the suppression of her better self.

The plot's last twist illustrates the incompatibility of Shen Teh and Shui Ta graphically. Shen Teh's 'absence' becomes so prolonged, that rumours spread that something has befallen her. She *has* to 'disappear', of course, because she is pregnant, and because Shui Ta's toughness is required to run the tobacco factory that is to provide for herself and the child. When Shen Teh's clothes are discovered, Shui Ta is arrested on a charge of murder. In one sense, the charge is justified, for it is only by suffocating the altruistic Shen Teh that Shui Ta has been able to save the business. At the climax of the trial, however, the 'bloated' businessman Shui Ta removes his disguise to reveal behind it the pregnant Shen Teh. The moral is conveyed visually: her swollen belly, focus of her love for Sun and for his child, is the reason for her transformation into Shui Ta.

The devices of the divine quest and the split character were the principal but not the sole means by which Brecht sought to lend his play the transparency of argument appropriate to dialectical theatre. The openly reflective character of the play was underlined by various forms of direct address to the audience. The water-seller, Wang, for example, opens the play by introducing himself and the conditions of life in Szechwan to the audience. This prologue is matched by an epilogue, spoken by an actor in front of the curtain, who apologises for the play's (apparent) failure to solve the problems it has raised:

> Should men be better? Should the world be changed?
> Or just the Gods? Or ought there to be none?
>
> (6i, 109)

and invites the audience to work out a solution for itself.

The main action is punctuated by a series of interludes, in which the Gods appear to Wang in dream to discuss with him the progress of events, and through songs. Compared with the unvarnished didacticism of Brecht's experiments at the beginning of the 1930s, where the audience was at times told quite plainly and directly what to think, the forms of address to the audience are mostly used rather more subtly in *The Good Person*. The epilogue's claim not to know the answer to the problems raised by the action is, of course, disingenuous, but the songs tend to function as a means of underlining a 'gestus' rather than of supplying ready-made formulae. Wang's 'Song of the water-seller in the Rain', for example, brings to the audience's attention the contradictions between his resentment, as a water-seller, of the rain (which reduces demand for his ware), and his natural joy, as a man who lives in a normally parched land, at the refreshing arrival of the rain. The song thus restates in concentrated form the conflict between nature and economic constraint that runs through the whole play.

This account of the dialectical-demonstrative character of *The Good Person of Szechwan* could be extended to cover many other features, of language and gesture, for example. However, such an analysis would still fall far short of giving a satisfactory account of the way Brecht's parable actually *works* in the theatre. Simply to 'shell out' the ideas incorporated in his plays is to undo or disregard the effects of the work of embodying abstractions in figures and situations which speak very directly, in their own right, to the imagination of the audience.

In this connection Brecht once made some interesting remarks to the critic Ernst Schumacher concerning the parable. Praising the fact that it presented the abstract concretely, Brecht called it 'the most cunning' of forms.[2] As an example he cited the case of Lenin, who once gained support for the Bolshevists' controversial New Economic Policy with the help of a short parable entitled 'On the Climbing of High Mountains', the moral of which seemed so self-evident to his audience 'that they simply swallowed the theoretical part of his argument whole' ('*daß sie das Theoretische mitgefressen haben*'). The 'cunning' of Lenin's parable lay in its substitution, by way of analogy, of a relatively simple problem for a much more complex and less clear-cut one, and also in its emotive, suggestive association of politics with the heroic activity of mountain climbing. Lenin's parable, in other words, was a classic instance of the rhetorical deployment of the imaginative qualities of the genre for purposes of persuasion. *The Good Person of Szechwan* is a more extended example of the same rhetorical procedures. Although the playwright makes a considerable show of the gestures of rational discourse, his 'case' depends heavily on various appeals to the emotions.

Brecht's parable makes the crucial assumption that human nature is fundamentally good. Yet this tenet of Marxist humanism is no scientifically demonstrable truth, but rather an article of faith. Indeed the Marxist concept of 'alienation' both asserts the existence of this human quality in nature, from which man has become separated through the evolution of culture, and makes such a quality undemonstrable by virtue of the processes that have supposedly corrupted it. Thus, if the spectator assents to the parable's assumptions about human nature, his willingness to 'suspend his disbelief' has no authority other than his own intuition of such a predisposition to goodness within himself, or his inclination to identify with this model of his innermost nature. To encourage identification with Shen Teh, Brecht makes her not merely good, but generous, gentle, warm, gifted with a sense of humour – and pretty as well. Any survey of productions of the play quickly shows how much its success in performance depends on the central role being played by an attractive young woman. Brecht's tendency to manipulate the spectator's conventional responses to physical types is equally evident in making the *fat* barber Shu Fu one of the villains of the piece. In production the physical attraction of Shen Teh also tends to be emphasised by its contrast with a range of negative physical qualities assigned to Shui Ta: angularity, hardness, the use of dark spectacles to hide the eyes. Such methods are the stock-in-trade of the popular artist, the cartoonist and the propagandist.

Shui Ta, like Shen Teh, is a character drawn from the repertoire of melodrama; 'he' is the type of the 'ruthless capitalist', she the 'innocent in distress'. Brecht's amalgamation of the two roles in a single, Jekyll-and-Hyde type

Melodrama

146

of character (without drugs or schizophrenia to facilitate the exchange of roles) would offend against common notions of psychological plausibility, if regarded naturalistically. However, Brecht was given considerable freedom to overstep the limits of probability by the genre in which he was working: because the audience is aware of the 'make believe' element in parable, it will tolerate a considerable degree of simplification, exaggeration or implausibility. Within this convention the 'character' is treated as if it were a psychological whole, and the 'hinge' that holds together the two halves of the character is an *emotional* one. The sight of Shen Teh being mercilessly exploited by those she has helped produces feelings of anger and the wish that she would defend herself. This desire to redress the balance is then satisfied by the appearance of Shui Ta, until, that is, 'he' goes too far, and the emotional balance tips in the opposite direction. The development of the role, in other words, presupposes an empathetic response from the audience. Without such identification some of Brecht's best effects would be entirely lost – when, for example, the audience has to add to the scene where Sun boasts to Shui Ta about Shen Teh's devotion to him, the *hidden*, ironic dimension that it is Shen Teh herself who is having to listen to these things. Similarly, Brecht's expectation that the stiff movements of Shui Ta will be understood as expressing the extent to which Shen Teh has to force herself to play the role of her cousin, illustrates his general reliance – even in a play that was not to be tainted with the 'opportunism' of *Galileo* – on the disdained empathetic method of Aristotelian theatre.

The simplification of reality characteristic of parable enabled Brecht to deploy the resources not only of melodrama but also those of farce, another 'simple' genre. The most obvious instance of this is his treatment of the

Melodrama Farce, genres

Gods. They have, as one might expect, a certain weight of abstract meaning to bear. These Gods reflect the moral and metaphysical assumptions that underpin the socio-economic *status quo* in Szechwan (the belief, for example, that powerful Gods exist, or that there are such things as absolute moral laws). Such 'ruling ideas', Marx argued, are the 'ideas of the rulers', derived from the social reality of exploitation and subordination, but designed both to deflect attention from that reality and to maintain it. Brecht was not interested in exploring dispassionately this view that morality and religion are mainly instruments of class hegemony. The play simply assumes the correctness of the view (the Gods are clearly confidence tricksters from the outset) and employs farce as a rhetorical device to encourage dissociation from the Gods (and hence from the ideas with which they are linked).

The initial appearance of the Gods amidst the misery of Szechwan, 'well-nourished, well-groomed and showing no signs of any employment', links them with the privileged classes and sets them up for the 'banana-skin' treatment they are to receive in the course of the play. After their first appearance in the flesh, their insubstantiality is then expressed by their appearing only in dream to Wang. The quality of farce is injected into these scenes by making their *gestus* of passing observers in the world of mortals repeatedly take on the character of a hasty and undignified flight from problems they cannot solve, until at last they float away on a rosy cloud, chanting a tercet and ignoring Shen Teh's desperate appeals for the help they cannot give. Their status as ineffectual clowns is also underlined by their increasingly dishevelled appearance and by the bruises they acquire in their wanderings through the real world. Brecht's definition of comedy as a technique which 'creates distance' is quite inadequate to account for the effects of such farce. Far from being a coolly intellectual form, it is one that involves the spectator vicariously in directing violence – the Gods' bruised heads are the evidence – against selected objects of antipathy. This is what the 'sovereign' attitude which epic/dialectical/scientific theatre was ostensibly designed to promote actually involved in practice.

Although it was a play of which he was fond and in which he had invested considerable time and effort, *The Good Person of Szechwan* was never produced by Brecht. Little is known about the contribution he made to the productions by Harry Buckwitz in Frankfurt (1952) or by Benno Besson in Rostock (1956), but his involvement does not appear to have been great in either case. The lack of a 'model' production stamped with Brecht's authority may account for the considerable range of interpretations this play has received. In principle Brecht was in favour of an independent approach to his plays (as his letter to Schweikart, who produced the play for the Schloßpark Theater in West Berlin, indicates); whether he would have approved of all the results is a quite different matter. Had Brecht produced the play himself, it is quite likely that he would have rewritten parts of the text, as he did while producing his other plays, for he tended to discover both new problems and new possibilities in characters and situations in the process of testing a play on stage; indeed he complained, while wrestling with the composition of *The Good Person*, that it was impossible for him to complete a play without a stage at his disposal on which to test out its theatrical viability (SM, 15). That he did not solve all the problems that presented themselves during the writing seems to be confirmed by the difficulties other producers have had in staging the play satisfactorily.

The West German premiere was in 1952 in Frankfurt

under the direction of Harry Buckwitz, who did much to promote Brecht's work in the BRD in the 1950s. His stage designer was Teo Otto, who had created the set for the première in Zürich some nine years previously. Otto's stage-design was non-naturalistic, an arrangement of vertical bamboo poles from which various drapes could be unfurled (for example, a black cloth to signify night) and which provided an easily variable playing-area. Buckwitz's direction, closely attentive to detail, aimed at an epic or 'documentary' statement, but nevertheless permitted a rise in emotional intensity in the course of the action on which critics, unhappy with the *longueurs* of the earlier scenes, seized with due gratitude. The production was credited with touching a 'social nerve', with being uncomfortable and acidic, but does not appear to have produced the effect Brecht generally aimed at, namely of teaching the spectator to perceive the social causes of problems and of encouraging a belief in their eradicability. Critics tended, rather, to see in the play a pessimistic, general account of the irreconcilability of goodness with the conditions of life in modern society (on both sides of the Iron Curtain) for which Brecht had no cure to offer. The epilogue's demand that the audience should find a happy ending was regarded as 'nothing more than a rhetorical effusion arising from a hopeless predicament' (SM, 143). The impression of pessimism arose from the play's depiction of human inadequacy as it parades through Shen Teh's little shop in various guises: the 'unfortunates, the loafers, the speculators, the greedy, etc.'. It may be that this reception reflects the failure of the production to apply Brechtian principles consistently, or it may reflect the inability of critics at that time to shake off their habitual way of looking at plays, but on the other hand it may equally well result from inherent features of the play text which arguably does not demonstrate the social causes of vice and virtue so unambiguously as to preclude such misinterpretation of Brecht's intentions.

Although Brecht attended and contributed to a few rehearsals of Hans Schweikart's production in Munich (1955) and even invited Schweikart to bring it to Berlin, this production of the play had even less bite and Brechtian toughness in performance than Buckwitz's. The result was a 'bittersweet parable of Shen Teh, the good prostitute' (SM, 152), permeated by an air of resigned, complete pessimism; the leading actress, who played Shen Teh in a gentle, lyrical style, had difficulty in handling the Shui Ta role. Successive actresses have found difficulty in doing justice to both halves of this double role. In part this may be because of its technical difficulty, but the roots of the problem reach deep down into the conception of the character itself. Even as he was writing the play Brecht was evidently troubled by the lack of consistency involved in presenting Shui Ta's 'badness' as being dictated by the logic of an exploitative social system, while allowing an unexplained exception to the rule of alienation in Shen Teh's ability to preserve her goodness in the midst of such degrading, normally dehumanising circumstances. The actress who can make Shen Teh's exceptional nature plausible is bound to have difficulty in making the audience believe that this same woman is capable of assuming the unscrupulous persona of Shui Ta at will.

The play received its première in the GDR with Benno Besson's first production of it in Rostock in 1956. In his determination to give the play more punch than in previous productions Besson went to the opposite extreme of stressing its didactic character and message with all the means at his disposal. However, in the judgement of Brecht's old supporter, the distinguished critic Herbert

Ihering, the producer's efforts were counterproductive. On the one hand, by surrounding the playing area with panels covered with political newspaper cuttings he had distracted attention from the poetic *words* at the heart of the imaginative world of the parable. On the other hand, Besson had allowed Käthe Reichel, in the role of Shen Teh, to inject too much pathos into her playing. Fritz Erpenbeck, less of an enthusiast for Brecht's theatre than Ihering, criticised the production along similar lines, namely for being so didactic as to fail to stimulate the spectator's capacity for independent thought and judgement. He felt there was a danger – even at this relatively early stage – that the lack of dogmatism in Brecht's own theatrical practice might disappear in the work of his disciples.[3]

In Ihering's judgement the faults of Besson's approach did not disappear when the production was transferred to the Berliner Ensemble in the following year: 'There could be no better proof for Brecht's own theory of Epic Theatre than this production, proof by way of antithesis. Brecht's language is dramatic, stageworthy and mimetic when it is spoken in an epic manner. As soon as it is forced to produce excited effects, its effectiveness disappears.' (SM, 162) Ihering's point is a good one, for Brecht's handling of language, character and situation is usually of such inherent affective power that it needs to be performed in an 'understating' manner (as in his own production of *Mother Courage*), so as not to appear sentimental, or overblown. As Brecht realised as early as 1920, the life of the drama is enhanced the more 'hostility', or clash of opposites, there exists amongst the elements in each scene. One of the chief sources of such 'hostility' in his work is the tension between powerfully emotive subject-matter and a 'cool' presentational style.

Besson's next production at the East Berlin Volksbühne in 1970 used even bolder means of expression, some of them borrowed from contemporary pop art, some from older traditions of popular culture, such as the enormous masks worn at carnival processions in the South of Germany, or a vertical arrangement of boxed-in playing areas reminiscent of the cubicles used on the medieval stage. All the characters, including Shen Teh, wore masks to show the deforming effect of living in this kind of society, but, as in Brecht's own production of *The Caucasian Chalk Circle*, the masks were of different kinds. The poor characters were given simple, soft, stocking masks which left the most expressive parts of the face (eyes and mouth) exposed. Characters whose greater wealth has caused them to lose more of their humanity, were given hard, pumpkin-like masks or, as in the case of the policeman, extra-large hands. The grotesque effect was further emphasised by stylisation of gesture and manner of speech. At the end the Gods, who wore huge head masks that gave their voices a hollow ring, did not retire to heaven on a rosy cloud but suddenly became insubstantial, three limp pieces of white cloth wafting up and out of sight.

In this production humanity was shown to be all but smothered as men struggled for survival on the neglected edge of a great, unfeeling modern city evidently located somewhere in South America. Plastic sheeting was stretched up the sides of the stage, in one corner of which lay Wang's abode – not a sewage pipe as Brecht had suggested, but a broken-down old car; whenever he dreamed of the Gods the stage was flooded with magical light. In this refuse-heap world the general brutality of the people was both plausible and, as a consequence of their material deprivation, understandable.

One result of Besson's experiment at the Volksbühne

seems to have been to make Manfred Wekwerth (now artistic director of the Berliner Ensemble) react strongly against that production when he came to direct it himself in Zürich in 1976. His Gods were no phantoms who appeared in dreams but were conceived as bourgeois intellectuals who came on to the stage, not from the wings or the flies, but from their seats in the auditorium. During their journey through the world, they descended the social ladder by stages, until they became tramps who seemed to have wandered in from a Beckett play. This permitted a sharp contrast with the final scene when the Gods were transformed, phoenix-like, into resplendent representatives of 'official optimism' before dissolving into insubstantiality. Except in this final scene, Wekwerth sought to avoid any impression of theatricality, such as the use of exaggerated masks, so as to confront the audience with the form of alienation with which they are so familiar as to be unaware of it – normal, everyday life under capitalism. This overall conception of the play led Wekwerth to present a quite different interpretation of Shui Ta from Brecht's. Instead of showing the difficulties arising for Shui Ta from the need to suppress Shen Teh's benevolent urges, Wekwerth thought of the 'male' role as completely relaxed, secure in the knowledge that all its actions are in accordance with the laws and morality of a world in which Shen Teh is a social misfit.

The Good Person of Szechwan is a play which evidently has held a particular fascination for some producers who have kept coming back to it, with new approaches to try out. One of these is Giorgio Strehler who has directed three different productions of it, the last of which, a co-operative undertaking shared by his own Piccolo Teatro and the Teatro Emilia Camagua, was acclaimed when he brought it to Berlin in 1981. Strehler originally made much of the fairy-tale qualities of the play, so as to draw the audience into a conflict between the desire to imagine the world as it might be and a recognition of the reasons why reality falls so far short of such ideal imaginings. In his last production Strehler retained this approach, but set the action more recognisably in contemporary Italy, without, however, making any concessions to naturalism in the performance. For the style of acting he drew heavily on the tradition of *commedia dell'arte*, insisting that his actors move as expressively as dancers, while at the same time augmenting the caricaturing tendency of popular farce (the policeman as *miles gloriosus*) with techniques drawn from slapstick and expressionist cinema. Thus Shui Ta, for example, was made to move like a robot, in a manner reminiscent of a gangster or the Golem. This stiff artificiality of movement helped convey a sense of the violence done to Shen Teh's nature by the adoption of Shui Ta's persona. But whereas this part of Andrea Jonasson's performance was a convincing embodiment of the stress of living in a harshly competitive society, her Shen Teh, beautiful, moving, clothed in a loose, flowing costume, remained a figure of fantasy.

To focus attention on the figures, Strehler had the action played against a bare cyclorama, with a minimum of properties on stage. Changes of locale and mood were created by carefully contrived lighting effects, in which the figures sometimes became silhouettes. The 'realistic' explanation for the diffuse light was the rainy climate of Szechwan and the dust from the cement factory in the neighbourhood, but the effect was to counterbalance the emotional vehemence of the action while yet giving sensuous, aesthetic expression to the loss of human substance occasioned by the conditions of life in the contemporary world. The floor of the stage gave the illusion of muddy ground covered with puddles, which not only helped motivate the various forms of movement that contributed to the characterisation (agile leaps, fastidious teetering on tip-toe) but also contributed to the symbolism: water, the essential of life, mixed with earth and cement-dust to produce dirty, unproductive mud. Although clearly much more atmospheric than any of Brecht's own productions, Strehler's ability to intensify the emotional impact of the play without prejudice to the clarity of the argument seems a quite legitimate development of Brechtian theatre and one which justifies Brecht's remark, in a letter to the still relatively young Strehler, that he would like to leave him the rights to perform his plays throughout Europe.

9
The Caucasian Chalk Circle

Now regarded as a classic example of Epic Theatre, *The Caucasian Chalk Circle* developed, ironically enough, from an invitation to Brecht arranged by the actress, Luise Rainer, to write a play she could perform on Broadway, a commission which prompted him to cast in theatrical form a story he had written some years previously ('The Augsburg Chalk Circle'). Initially the commission inspired him with little enthusiasm 'in this empty place, devoid of wishes'. Only a week after sending off the completed manuscript to Rainer, Brecht suddenly felt dissatisfied with the concessions he had made to the audience's presumed taste for idealised heroines:

> Suddenly I am no longer content with Grusha in *The Caucasian Chalk Circle*. She should be simple-minded, look like Brueghel's *Dulle Griet*, a beast of burden. She should be mulish rather than uppity, willing rather than good, have stamina rather than incorruptibility, etc., etc. This simplicity should on no account signify 'wisdom'

(that is the familiar cliché), although it is quite compatible with a practical disposition, even with cunning and an
eye for human qualities. Grusha, by being stamped with
the backwardness of her class, should invite less identification, and thus present objectively a figure who in a
certain sense is tragic ('the salt of the earth').

(KM, 23)

Brecht revised the text in an attempt to meet his own
objections. These revisions did not, however, succeed in
reducing Grusha's attractiveness as a figure of identification to anything like the extent he once thought was
necessary. As John Willett has observed, 'he does not seem
to have altered her much or provided those practical
motives for her goodness which Feuchtwanger (who
thought her "too holy") has asked for' (7, 214). If anything,
the changes, by emphasising the part played by Grusha's
simple-mindedness in her getting 'landed' with someone
else's child, made her more rather than less moving.
Despite its many 'epic' features, the finished play makes
powerful emotional appeals which are not basically dissimilar from those made by the products of Broadway or
Hollywood.

The scenes telling the ancient story of Grusha and the
'high-born child' are made into a play within a play by being
preceded by a scene set in the contemporary world, entitled
'The Struggle for the Valley', and followed by an epilogue
pointing a moral that applies equally to the ancient case and
the modern one. Two peasant collectives from Georgia in
the Soviet Union are in dispute about which one has the
better claim to a valley. One is a group of goat-herdsmen
who used to graze their flocks here until they were driven
away by the invading German army. The other group want
to develop the land for fruit-farming, proposing to irrigate

it with the help of a new reservoir. In Brecht's original conception of the play the dispute was to be settled with the aid of the play within the play, the ancient case demonstrating the principle that greater productivity constitutes a better claim to the land than traditional rights of possession. In the final version of the play the dispute is settled by amicable discussion before the play within the play is performed, so that this now has the character of a celebration of the wisdom of the people in reaching their agreement. If the original version exemplified Brecht's idea of practical, 'interventionist' (*eingreifendes*), problem-solving theatre, the revised version illustrates the more general conception of aesthetic education elaborated in the *Short Organum for the Theatre*.

Friedrich Schiller, the most famous German exponent of aesthetic education, once drew a distinction between two types of writing or writer: the 'sentimental', by which he meant a reflective, self-aware and self-questioning type, and the 'naïve' type, such as is found in heroic poetry, where the shared values of writer and audience are treated as unproblematic. Brecht implicitly rejected any such distinction by arguing for and practising a form of theatre that was 'naïve' while at the same time addressing itself to the audience's capacity for reflection. Naïveté as Brecht understood it was firstly a matter of not pretending that the stage was anything but a stage, of rejecting the naturalistic assumption that, say, a crowd needed to be represented by a stage full of extras. But Brecht's theatre was also naïve in the Schillerian sense in that it laid claim to a clear and firm set of human and political values which it propounded in a partisan way. Communism, as Brecht put it, was 'the simple thing that is difficult to achieve' (*'Das Einfache, das schwer zu machen ist'*) (GW2, 852).

Brecht's liking for the 'naïve' is embodied in the person

of Arkadi Cheidse, 'The Singer', described as 'a sturdy man of simple manners' who has the task of directing the play to be performed by the peasants. The characterisation of this figure reflects his status as a representative of the tradition of folk poetry and repository of ancient wisdom with which Brecht wanted to see his own work aligned. Naïve, too, are the forms in which the scenes of the Singer's epic poem are dramatised: the story of Grusha frequently has the quality of secularised legend, while that of Azdak recalls the farcical adventures of a German folk-hero, the prankster Till Eulenspiegel. Brecht asked his designer, Karl von Appen, to bring out the folksy, primitive quality of the fable in the grouping and costumes of the figures – for example, by making the seams on robes raised and apparently clumsy, just as they are on the figures in Nativity scenes (*Krippenszenen*) in rural churches.

The motivation for all this naïveté lies partly in the fact that the peasants of the prologue live in a country where feudalism still survived until quite recently, indeed until within living memory. The other justification for the naïveté of the peasants' play about Grusha and Azdak lies in the fact of the Russian Revolution, an event that has brought the wheel of history full circle, so to speak, emancipating men from class-structures and enabling them to start building history anew by re-shaping social life according to natural, though long forgotten principles. From the point of view of what is assumed to be a qualitatively new way of life, the centuries when all history was the history of class struggle seem to belong to quite another epoch, so that the long historical process of class antagonism, because it supposedly no longer enmeshes the lives of these Soviet citizens, can be simplified to the point where it becomes the stuff of ballad, legend and farce.

While the fiction that the play within the play is based on

an old folk epic or ballad creates a framework of convention within which the simplifications of the parable-like tale of Grusha and Azdak might be made acceptable to a modern audience, the account of contemporary history offered by the introductory 'Struggle for the Valley' is naïve in a merely negative sense, if not downright disingenuous. The real history of Soviet agricultural collectivisation was one of coercion and resistance. Whereas the peasants in Brecht's play relinquish the valley that was their home after only the mildest of protests, so seduced are their minds by the 'sly' plans for irrigation, for many Russian peasants the loss of their homelands was a matter of being herded into cattle-trucks and forcibly deported (if they survived the journey) to some distant corner of the Soviet territory. Not surprisingly, the Utopian prologue, unconvincing wherever it is performed, simply has to be omitted in any Russian production.

As one would expect from a play making extensive use of naïve dramatic forms, *The Caucasian Chalk Circle* is rich in emotive effects.[1] The main focus of the play's emotional appeal is, of course, the maid Grusha. Even before she decides to take responsibility for the baby that has been abandoned in the panic of a palace revolution by everyone else, including its mother, Grusha is presented in an attractive light in two scenes where she is first teased and then proposed to by the soldier Simon. Her attraction resides in a directness and honesty of feeling that seems to be a beneficial consequence of the fact that she is rather naïve and not very quick on the uptake – though she is not lacking in good sense, as her warning to Simon against any unnecessary heroics makes clear.

In the last scene of the first act, when she finally picks up the abandoned child and goes off with it in search of a refuge, the emotive effect has been carefully built up by the preceding scenes. In them the audience has seen how the child's mother, wife of the city governor, simply forgets about her baby in her concern first to select which clothes she will take with her and then with her own safety; that the other servants, including the child's nurse, are as ruthless as Natella Abashvili in putting their own interests first and simply abandoning 'the brat' to its fate rather than risk being caught with a child whom the new masters will want to kill; how a group of soldiers under the command of the 'Fat Prince' carry in on the point of a lance the severed head of the governor and impale it above the palace gate. It even seems for a moment that Grusha too, after wrapping the child in some of Natella's abandoned clothes and bedding it down amongst the luggage, is going to follow the advice and example of the other servants. However, just as she is on the point of leaving, she hears the child, through the voice of the Singer, 'speaking' to her and asking for her help. It is of course her conscience telling her that she will never again know peace of mind if she ignores the plight of the child:

The child
Called to her, not whining but calling quite sensibly
At least so it seemed to her: 'Woman', it said,
'Help me'.
Went on calling not whining but calling quite sensibly:
'Don't you know, woman, that she who does not listen to a cry for help
But passes by shutting her ears, will never hear
The gentle call of a lover
Nor the blackbird at dawn, nor the happy
Sigh of the exhausted grape-picker at the sound of the Angelus. (7, 164)

Grusha then spends the night watching over the child, fetching milk for it and keeping it warm, while around her the city is filled with flames and the tumult of civil war. By daybreak she finds – as the audience has already hoped and guessed – that she has sat too long:

> Too long she sat, too long she watched
> The soft breathing, the little fists
> Till towards morning the temptation grew too
> strong.   (7, 165)

The emotional bond forged between Grusha, the child and the audience in the first act is strengthened as the action unfolds. She leaves the city and sets off for the Northern Mountains, hoping to find shelter for herself and the child with her brother who has married into a relatively rich farm. During the journey she encounters one difficulty or danger after another, each situation throwing her human worth into ever clearer relief. She has to pay an extortionate sum (half a week's wages) from her very meagre means to buy just one drink of milk for Michael, and is willing to pay an even more outrageous sum, equivalent to ten weeks' pay, just to have some shelter for Michael at night from the icy winds coming down from the Janga Tau glacier – and at the same time to be exposed to the heartlessness of a pair of aristocratic women refugees.

The greatest threat to Grusha and the child comes from two soldiers who are pursuing them in order to gain the reward on the child's head. Utterly exhausted by the forced march into the mountains burdened with the weight of the child, Grusha decides at one point that the best thing for both of them is for her to leave the child at the door of a peasant cottage. Once she sees that Michael has been carried into the hut by the woman, Grusha sets off in the opposite direction, laughing at the success of her ploy and pleased to be free of a burden that had become too great for her, yet deeply saddened at the loss of the child.

This was one of the points where Brecht wanted to make it clear that Grusha's relationship with the child is not one of simple saintliness. She still has interests of her own, separate from and even at odds with those of Michael, for she has another, older attachment, to the soldier Simon, and wants to be free to find him when the civil war is over. On the other hand, it is evident that she can only bring herself to leave Michael because it seems in the child's best interests: she fears that she cannot go on fleeing fast enough to keep ahead of their pursuers, and believes that Michael stands a better chance of survival in the unlikely hiding-place of a distant peasant cottage. In the end, though, this attempt at separation functions as a kind of emotional 'retardation' which has the effect, not of reducing but of intensifying the forward thrust of the action towards an ever closer emotional identification between the woman and the child. Grusha has hardly gone a few steps when she runs into the pursuing *Panzerreiter* (Iron-shirts or armoured cavalrymen), and, questioned as to the whereabouts of the missing child, flees in panic back to the hut, thereby leading them unintentionally to the child. In a scene of ever rising emotional suspense the soldier in command comes close to taking possession of the child, and is only prevented from doing so by Grusha's desperate courage in attacking him with a block of wood.

This is not an isolated case of Brecht's use of conventional dramatic suspense in the play. Having adopted the child as her own by substituting rags for its fine linen and baptising it with glacier water (a symbolic initiation into the harshness of a poor person's life), Grusha has to risk both their lives crossing a chasm spanned by a primitive bridge with rotten boards and one broken guide-rope. To make matters worse, the light is waning and a storm is blowing up. Grusha makes it across, of course, her courage being emphasised (as it was in the scene in the peasant hut) by contrast with the passivity of some merchants encamped by the bridge and the cowardice of her pursuers. The scene could have been taken straight from a Hollywood adventure movie (in fact, as Brecht was an avid film-goer, this may well have been its inspiration).

A whole range of different emotive effects is employed in Act Three, which deals with Grusha's experiences once she has reached the farmstead in the Northern Mountains where her brother lives. Even here her sufferings and problems are far from being at an end. When Grusha enters the farmhouse she is so weak and ill that she can barely stand unaided. Yet the response of her well-fed sister-in-law, who completely dominates her husband, is suspicious to the point of hostility, for she sees in Grusha, whom she takes to be the mother of an illegitimate child, merely a threat to her own respectability (she is 'pious', as the brother explains) and a drain on the resources of her household. Here, as so often in the play, those who could best afford to help prove to be the least willing to do so. When Grusha collapses during the sister-in-law's interrogation her brother is about to carry her to the bench by the stove but his wife orders him instead to let her lie on a sack by the wall. The scene exploits the audience's sympathetic identification with Grusha in the same way as countless similar scenes in popular melodrama, a tradition that survived into the twentieth century principally in the shape of the 'tear-jerker' type of film; despite his general show of cynicism the young Brecht confessed to having been deeply affected by one of Chaplin's contributions to this genre, a film entitled *Alcohol and Love*.[2]

In subsequent scenes Brecht uses effects of emotional dissonance to bring home Grusha's plight to the audience. As long as the mountain passes are blocked by snow she and Michael are allowed to stay at the farm – provided they eat little, make no complaints about the cold and provided Grusha works hard for the sister-in-law. Once the spring comes, however, bringing with it the danger that her pursuers will come here to find her, the brother insists on arranging a marriage for Grusha. During the scene when he announces this plan the air is filled with the increasingly regular sound of drops of water melting from the ice on the roof of the barn (an effect rendered symbolically by a *glockenspiel*), so as to produce conflicting emotional associations of beauty and release from the miseries of winter on the one hand and of the combined threat to Grusha's happiness presented by the pursuing soldiers and the unwanted husband on the other.

Grusha, still faithful to Simon, only agrees to her brother's plan because she is assured that the marriage will be merely a formality to gain respectability and legitimising papers for the child and herself, in that the intended husband is already on his death-bed. The ensuing marriage scene, grotesque enough to begin with, turns into outright farce when the 'dying' man, on hearing that the war is over, gets up from his bed and shoos away the guests: it turns out that he has only been shamming to avoid being called-up. Yet the comic aspect of the scene is intermingled disturbingly with an aspect bordering on the tragic. As the guests chatter about the end of the war, attention is focused on Grusha's deeply distressed reaction to this most untimely reminder of Simon and her promise to wait for him until he returns from the war. Soon she is to experience still greater distress, however, for when Simon eventually comes to find her at the farm the tense emotions of both of them make it impossible for her to explain to him the true state of affairs. As they stand facing each other on opposite sides of a stream, hostile soldiers appear with Michael in their possession. In a last, desperate attempt to prevent Michael's abduction Grusha has to claim, in Simon's presence, that she is the boy's mother – to no avail. The child is taken away and Grusha can only run after the disappearing soldiers. Having risked her love for Simon to save Michael, it now appears that her reward is to lose both of them. Thus the main part of Grusha's story ends on a note of high suspense as to the outcome for Grusha and Michael. This sense of an incomplete emotional pattern means that the audience keeps the fate of Grusha and Michael in their minds as the Singer turns their attention to the story of Azdak, the judge who is to decide between the competing claims on Michael of Grusha, his adoptive mother, and the biological mother, Natella Abashvili.

Whereas Grusha's story mainly employed effects of sentiment, heroism or pathos (with occasional touches of comedy) to draw the audience into her struggle to behave humanely in a society where the majority of men of all classes are alienated from their own humanity by conflicts of material interest, the tale of Azdak the judge relies mainly on comedy (with occasional touches of pathos) to evoke sympathy for a rather different, less self-sacrificing approach to the defence of humane values in a hostile world.

Originally, Brecht had intended Azdak to be a thoroughly 'Till Eulenspiegel' or Schweykian type of character, a knave and a fool whose rulings, when he is elevated from village clerk to judge, result in something resembling justice quite by accident, as a by-product of his pursuit of fun and self-gratification. In the event, however, Brecht's Azdak did not turn out to be utterly 'self-centred, amoral and parasitic (. . .) the lowest, most depraved judge there has ever been'. (KM, 22) Rather, as Brecht later reminded the actor taking this role, he is 'a man of utterly unblemished character, a disappointed revolutionary who plays the part of a man gone to the dogs, just as in Shakespeare wise men play the part of fools'. (KM, 94)

The good heart beneath the gruff exterior (although vehemently denied by Azdak) is the first thing to be revealed about the man when he is introduced giving shelter to a fugitive. Admittedly, when Azdak recognises from the fugitive's manner that the man he is sheltering comes from the upper classes, his own class-consciousness (which is much more developed than Grusha's) makes him inclined to throw the man out, but in fact he cannot bring himself to hand over someone in terror of his life to the police, even if he is an aristocrat. On discovering that he has thereby spared the life of the hated Grand Prince, however, Azdak rushes into the city to confess his guilt before the popular revolutionary forces whom he falsely assumes to have seized power. Yet even here his behaviour is dictated at least as much by a human motive as it is by respect for the principles of class-struggle; in this case the human aspect is his wish to save his own neck by throwing himself on the mercy of the revolution:

(He acts with expansive gestures, looking sideways at the Ironshirts.)
'Out of ignorance I let the Grand Swindler escape. Tear me to pieces, brothers!' So as to get in first. (7, 204–5)

Although the soldiers he addresses are not the arm of a proletarian revolution, but merely mercenaries of the new aristocratic masters who have just bloodily suppressed an uprising amongst the carpet weavers, they decide to appoint Azdak in place of the judge they have just hanged. Their motives, too, are a mixture of class-resentment of those whose inept decisions they have to carry out, enjoyment of the power given them by their importance in a situation of civil war, dislike of and admiration for this upstart, ragged village clerk: 'The Judge was always a rascal. Now the rascal shall be the Judge.' (7, 212)

During this period in the office of judge, with which he has been 'landed' much as Grusha was with responsibility for Michael, Azdak holds the sympathy of the audience by virtue of the amusing, witty way he combines self-interest (always at the cost of the better-off) with concern to provide a modicum of justice for those brought before him. Because the palace revolution has not brought about the onset of a 'new age', but merely an age of 'new masters', Azdak realises that he cannot act on the basis of a new conception of justice, but must simply adapt to his own purposes the existing legal system. His way of proceeding is dialectical, exemplifying what Brecht defined as 'the negation of a negation'; because the existing laws are designed to protect the interests of the property-owning classes, Azdak always finds in favour of those who have none, basing himself on the assumption that the ultimate cause of the 'crimes' brought before him is to be found in the inequitable distribution of wealth in society. Until a revolution has created conditions in which there is no longer any fundamental conflict of interest between an individual or section of society and society at large (as in the 'Struggle for the Valley'), Azdak's rough class-justice is the best his individual reason can make of a society founded on unreasonable principles.

If the audience's sympathies for Azdak are angled for throughout by such details as his habit of sitting on the law-book and drinking good red wine while delivering judgement, or the sentimental scene where he places an old peasant woman on the judge's seat, these sympathies are most fully gratified in the final act of the play, when Azdak has to decide whether Michael should go to Grusha or Natella Abashvili. It is quite clear that Natella is only interested in recovering her own child because he is heir to his father's property, whereas Grusha wants to keep the boy, at least for a few years longer, because she wants to help him grow up healthy, happy and useful to others.

Although instinctively predisposed towards Grusha simply because she is a poor working woman, Azdak decides to put this intuitive sympathy to the test by subjecting the woman to the ancient trial of the chalk circle. The child has to stand in the middle and the competing 'mothers' are to try to pull him out on one side or the other. The test is made twice, and twice it is Natella who pulls Michael out of the circle, not because she is physically stronger, but because Grusha cannot bring herself to hurt Michael by making him the object of a tug-of-war. In finding that the test has proved Grusha to be the true mother of Michael, Azdak acts in accordance with the traditional trial of the chalk circle, except in one fundamental respect: the woman whom he recognises to be the 'true' mother is not the one who gave birth to the child but the one who 'stole' the child and *became* its mother by virtue of what she has done for it. Underlying this judgement is Brecht's Marxist belief that, unlike other animals, man's life is not principally defined or to be judged in biological terms, but as a process of self-creation or productivity. For Azdak the past therefore carries weight only in as much as it is relevant to the future: he does not decide which woman has the better *right* to 'possess' the child, but bases his judgement on the child's right to a good mother, and so grants Grusha the *privilege* of bearing the responsibility for Michael's further upbringing. Nevertheless, the audience is bound to regard the verdict as a reward for the hardships Grusha has suffered on behalf of Michael. Like all happy endings, it brings to a satisfying conclusion the emotional curve of the action.

The emotive quality of Brecht's construction of character and plot was reinforced by features of staging and performance in his own production of the play for the Berliner Ensemble, a production which won critical acclaim at the Paris Theatre festival in 1955, and subsequently in other capitals. Angelika Hurwicz's acting of the role of Grusha, for example, was generally felt to be very moving: 'Angelika Hurwicz plays the part for long stretches with all the means of the dramatic theatre. She affects us deeply. At times she is breathtakingly magnificent' (Fritz Erpenbeck)[3]; 'a powerful, moving impression is produced by Angelika Hurwicz's exceedingly sensitive, vigorous embodiment of Grusha's beautiful motherliness' (Hermann Martin).[4] Ernst Busch's interpretation of Azdak, similarly, was felt to be 'a figure bursting with life to an uncommon degree' and one in which full rein was given to this actor's 'markedly individual temperament' (Peter Edel).[5]

One of the means whereby Brecht caused Grusha in particular to be a focus of emotional attention was his use of masks. These masks are frequently cited as an example of Brecht's alienation effect, which they certainly were, in the sense that they signalled in an obviously allegorical manner the emotional rigidity and reduced (that is to say, socially alienated) humanity of those wearing them – the upper classes and their lackeys. At the same time as being intellectually apprehended signs, however, these masks had a tactile-emotive suggestiveness that was emphasised through contrast with the naked, natural faces of those characters for whom the play arouses sympathy. As well as representing the cruelty of the powerful by means of similar devices of stylisation to those employed by Walt Disney (Natella Abashvili's mask strongly recalls the face of the Wicked Queen in *Snow White*), the hard, stiff material of the masks forms part of a pattern of contrasts between hardness and softness running through the play: between the soft, thin, close-fitting dress worn by Grusha and the heavy, stiff robes worn by the Governor and his wife (repeated in the contrast of Michael's original shawl with the rags in which Grusha dresses him); between the armour of the soldiers or 'Ironshirts' and the flesh of Grusha, exposed when she vainly tries to still Michael by suckling him at her empty breast; between the heavy judicial robes and the thin rags Azdak still wears beneath them (emphasised in the 1976 Ensemble production by Ekkehard Schall's repeated exposure of his naked backside); between coins and milk; between ice and flowing water. Such contrasts are connotative as well as denotative, enhancing the appeal of the vulnerably human by focusing on its isolation in a world dominated by alien things – money and the weapons needed to gain or keep possession of it.

The allusion to crib scenes of Mary with the infant Jesus implied in the staging of the night-scene where Grusha watches over the baby, is similarly part of a symbolic, associative and emotive pattern running through the play. It exemplifies what Brecht defined as the *Umfunktionierung* of tradition, a process of taking over traditional material and assigning some new function, significance or value to it. In this case Brecht was offering the story of Grusha and Michael as a humanist re-fashioning of the Christian account of the 'Holy Family', interpreting the origin of the 'High-Born Child' in social terms, and stressing the working-class nature of the 'lowly' condition into which he is pitched and the inherent worth and dignity of a simply human life founded on work and human warmth in need of no transcendent associations to magnify it. At the same time, however, Brecht was thereby mobilising a traditionally ingrained awe of 'pure motherhood' to reinforce the impact Grusha has on the audience. Much the same is true of numerous allusions to Christ's Passion in the story of Azdak – mocking soldiers dress him in a travesty of a judge's (king's) dress. He is reviled by them and prepared for execution, and asks for a drink (in this case red wine) to ease his suffering – so that his ill-treatment acquires a greater weight of pathos, becoming a symbol of man's repeated inhumanity to other 'sons of men'.

This analysis, which could be extended to cover other expressive features of the play such as the at times pathetic language, should suffice to demonstrate that the basis of Brecht's rhetorical strategy in *The Caucasian Chalk Circle* was an appeal to the spectator's emotions – including the 'fear and pity' of Aristotelian drama. Having established this, however, one has to consider the contribution made to the overall effect of the play by its epic, alienating, or non-illusionistic features: the interventions of the Singer to direct or comment on the actions of the characters or to describe their feelings as they themselves stand silent; the light, stylised sets such as the backdrops after the manner of Chinese brush-drawings; the concentrated, paradoxical language used by the Singer and sometimes by Azdak (a link stressed by Brecht's choice of Ernst Busch to play both parts in his production) – lines such as 'Terrible is the temptation to do good' or the exchange of proverbs between Simon and Azdak in the court-room, for example, ' "I love you like a father," said the Czar to the peasants, and had the Czarevitsch's head chopped off.'

Devices like this need not necessarily reduce the emotional impact of a play. Audiences can adapt very quickly to different, even mixed conventions (consider pantomime, for example, where narration and action, burlesque and sentiment can co-exist perfectly happily), and intellectual clarification is far from being incompatible with emotive power: 'Terrible is the temptation to do good' strikes the heart as well as the mind. On the other hand, when Brecht's production of the play was first presented to the public, it was evident that he had put obstacles in the way of the spectator's quick adaptation to his mix of conventions.

The East German critic, Fritz Erpenbeck, for example, who confessed to being impressed and moved by some aspects of the play, was disturbed by what seemed to be its stylistic inconsistency, as when Angelika Hurwicz's playing of Grusha would suddenly change from being passionate to dispassionate: 'She suddenly freezes; the Singer informs the audience of what she is thinking. Or she will deliver her lines in a consciously monotonous manner – narrating like some other person standing by the side of the character. Or, directly before a passage that leads us to expect supreme human pathos, she will suddenly and deliberately shut off all emotion in order to report soberly on her emotion. That is an aesthetic contradiction.'[6] Erpenbeck went on to explain that he could accept and enjoy a consistently stylised type of presentation, such as he was familiar with in the theatre of the Far East, or one that was consistently realistic and direct in its emotional appeal. What irritated him in Brecht's production of *The Chalk Circle*, because he was unable to perceive the purpose it served, was the hard, unmediated juxtaposition of heterogeneous theatrical conventions.

Brecht had, of course, a conscious reason for not wanting to supply the kind of aesthetic consistency expected and demanded by Erpenbeck. He wanted to inhibit any tendency on the part of the spectator to watch a play from within the security of a familiar, convention-governed set of expectations, believing that this tended to reduce experience in the theatre to mere theatrical experience, something that was kept in a separate compartment from other kinds and areas of experience. One of Brecht's early reflections on the theatre expresses his ambition to engage the spectator with the *substance* of a play rather than its style, and outlines a strategy for achieving this end:

Once I get my hooks on a theatre I shall hire two clowns. They will perform in the interval and pretend to be spectators. They will bandy opinions about the play and about the members of the audience. Make bets on the outcome. (. . .) For tragedies the scene-changes will take place with the curtain up. Clowns will stroll across the stage, giving orders (. . .) The clowns will laugh about any hero as about a private individual. Absurd incidents, anecdotes, jokes. (. . .) The idea would be to bring reality back to the things on the stage. For God's sake, it's the *things* that need to be criticised – the action, words, gestures – not their execution.

(D, 32)

Two critics, Christiane Kaemmel and Alfred Voelkel, who were evidently familiar with and sympathetic to Brecht's intentions defended the use of this type of technique in *The Chalk Circle* production:

The dramatic tension of the action is so powerful that its interruption by the Singer is felt as a brutal intrusion. This brutality is, however, appropriate and indeed necessary: one is forced thereby to pay attention to the motives and consequences of the actions performed on stage. The spectator is freed from a purely subjective participation in the characters' experience and returned to the position of an objective observer. The Singer interprets a sequence of events which already belong to the past. In this way the direct impact of the play is inhibited in order to profile the issues more sharply.[7]

It would be to overlook a genuine problem, however, if one were simply to accept this defence of Brecht's practice (on the basis of Brecht's own theories) and to dismiss Erpenbeck's objections as those of a traditionalist unwilling to open his mind to new departures in the theatre. Whatever one thinks of Erpenbeck, it has to be noted that he was not alone in voicing such criticisms of the production. Hermann Martin, too, felt that 'the epic element has become disproportionately strong', while Peter Edel was disturbed by the *erklügelt* (cerebral, over-elaborate, lacking in spontaneity) impression made by the style of direction. Friedrich Luft, a leading critic from West Berlin, although favourably impressed by previous visits to the Ensemble, argued in a similar vein that Brecht's work had gone off the rails in this instance:

Whereas in earlier productions a refreshing and clarifying effect resulted from a fruitful cooling-down of the manner of presentation, Brecht is now labouring away as if in a refrigerator, utterly unmindful of his public. Clearly quite isolated, he has lost his way. This production has been rehearsed and worked-over for nigh on a year. The result is something artificial, pernickety and overdone, and is therefore boring in a very exhausting way – for four whole hours.[8]

It is clear, then, that the effect intended by Brecht's

alienation devices, that of concentrating critical attention on the *substance* of the play was not necessarily the effect they actually produced. In fact the effect could be the very opposite: the devices evidently struck some spectators as obtrusive, attracting attention to themselves rather than to the matters at issue. The reason why this problem became particularly acute in *The Caucasian Chalk Circle* is to be found, I believe, in the fact that the alienation devices, particularly when employed in scenes involving Grusha, had little to bite on. Although Brecht tried to point to the contradictions in her behaviour, these are relatively weak in comparison with the contradictions in the lives of Mother Courage or Galileo; Grusha was simply cast in too ideal a mould, and was too naïve a character, to throw much light on the conflicts generated by life in a class-society. It is also striking that Brecht particularly tended to intervene with commentary from the Singer in scenes depicting emotions of a tender nature. Apart from some personal aversion on Brecht's part to the direct depiction of emotions of this kind, Erpenbeck is surely right in saying that the reasons for the intervention of the Singer at some of these moments are neither obvious nor compelling.

A further difficulty arising from Brecht's alienating interruptions of the dramatic flow was a loss of tempo in a play that was already unusually long. In consequence, there was a tendency for the spectator to lose the thread and a sense of the epic whole to which the individual scenes contributed: 'Because of all these distractions (. . .) I lost sight of the threads of the two main plots which are only joined up in the final scene.' (Hermann Martin)

It seems, then, that Brecht was counting his chickens before they were hatched when he observed during work on the play: 'It is of course our new public that permits and obliges us to aim at precisely those effects which rest on a natural unity of thought and feeling.' (KM, 98). Ever the pragmatist, however, Brecht considerably modified the production before bringing it to the Paris theatre festival: he cut it, speeded up the tempo, aimed at a smoother flow, urged Paul Dessau to make the accompanying music simpler and less 'strenuous' (it had originally attracted much criticism for being distracting), and reduced the sharpness of the clash between the dramatic action and the Singer's interventions. The result appears to have been theatre that *worked*, (although not, of course, in the view of everybody), a production that won sympathy for Azdak's cunning on behalf of the poor (including himself!) and for the hardworking Grusha's good-hearted capacity for self-sacrifice. This was a far cry from the fierce criticisms of failure to behave in a consistently class-conscious manner which Brecht had made in a number of plays in the early 1930s. In the end, however, it may well have been a more effective way of gaining support for *die gute Sache* (the good cause) of working-class solidarity to which he had devoted so much of his life.

Notes

1. Introduction: Life and Works

1. See *Brecht in Augsburg*, ed. W. Frisch and K. W. Obermeier (Berlin and Weimar, 1975), p. 33.

2. The most recent evidence of this kind has been supplied by Ruth Berlau (one of Brecht's numerous lovers) in her memoirs, *Brechts Lai-Tu. Erinnerungen und Notate von Ruth Berlau*, ed. H. Bunge (Darmstadt, 1985).

3. For two contrasting accounts of Brecht's juvenilia see Reinhold Grimm, 'Brecht's Beginnings', *The Drama Review*, vol. 12, no. 1 (1967), pp. 22–35, and R. C. Speirs, 'Brecht from the beginning', *German Life and Letters*, XXXV, no. 1 (1981), pp. 37–46.

4. The line 'Cover your tracks' is the refrain of the first poem in Brecht's 'Reader for those who live in Cities' (P, 130–1).

5. Brecht's development has been much discussed. Two interesting essays on this topic are: P. Heller, 'Nihilist into Activist. Two phases in the Development of Bertolt Brecht', *Germanic Review*, vol. 28 (1953), pp. 144–55, and W. Steer, '*Baal*: a Key to Brecht's Communism', *German Life and Letters*, vol. 19 (1965–6), pp. 40–51.

6. Brecht defined the aim of these playlets thus: 'The presenters of these pieces, both actors and singers, have the task of learning as they teach' (GW 17, p. 1032).

7. See E. Piscator, *The Political Theatre*, trans. H. Rorrison (London, 1980).

179

8. See the poem 'Concerning the label emigrant' (P, p. 301).

9. See David Pike, *German Writers in Soviet Exile, 1933–45* (Chapel Hill, 1982) and David Pike, *Lukács and Brecht* (Chapel Hill, 1985).

2. The Plays of the Twenties

1. See Fritz Sternberg, *Der Dichter und die Ratio* (Göttingen, 1963), p. 67.

2. *Klingsors letzter Sommer* (Zurich, n.d.), p. 276.

3. *Baal. Der böse Baal, der Asoziale* (Frankfurt a.M., 1968), p. 99.

4. These lines from the first (1918) version of the play were omitted when Brecht revised it. See *Baal. Drei Fassungen*, ed. D. Schmidt (Frankfurt a.M., 1969), p. 55.

5. See Herbert Jhering, *Von Reinhardt bis Brecht*, vol. 1 (Berlin, 1958), p. 273.

6. These lines from the first edition of the play (Drei Masken Verlag, Munich, 1922) were among those altered in subsequent editions (cf. Methuen vol. 1, p. 114).

7. ibid, p. 94.

8. See the notes headed 'Materialwert' in GW 15, p. 105 et seq.

9. See Arrigo Subiotto, *Bertolt Brecht's Adaptations for the Berliner Ensemble* (London, 1975).

10. Herbert Jhering, *Die Zwanziger Jahre* (Berlin, 1948), p. 166.

11. These notes are taken from an unpublished record by Brecht of the production in the keeping of the Bertolt Brecht Archive (BBA 329/22).

12. ibid.

13. ibid.

14. See S. McDowell, 'Actors on Brecht: the Munich Years', *The Drama Review*, vol. 20, no. 3 (1976), pp. 101–16.

15. ibid, p. 115.

16. *Brecht in der Kritik*, ed. M. Wyss (Munich, 1977), pp. 47–8.

3. Theories of Theatre

1. 'sorge, daß meine Effekte (poetischer und philosophischer Art) auf die Bühne begrenzt bleiben' (GW 15, p. 62). Willett renders this (incorrectly) as 'have ensured, that the stage realisation of my (poetical and philosophical) effects remains within bounds' (D, p. 159).

2. For a discussion of this topic, see David Pike, *Lukács and Brecht* (Chapel Hill, 1985).

3. BBA 448/80.

4. Brecht's Practice of Theatre

1. Carl Weber, 'Brecht as Director', *The Drama Review*, vol. 12, no. 1 (1967), p. 103.

2. ibid, p. 103.

3. Marieluise Fleißer, 'Aus der Augustenstraße', in *50 Jahre Schauspielhaus, München* (1951).

4. *Materialien zu Brechts 'Leben des Galilei'* (Frankfurt a.M., 1968), p. 119.

5. Carl Weber, 'Brecht as Director' (see above), p. 101.

6. CM, p. 244.

7. 'Dialogue: Berliner Ensemble', *The Drama Review*, vol. 12, no. 1 (1967), pp. 114–15.

8. E. Bentley, *The Brecht Commentaries, 1943–80* (New York, 1981), p. 61.

9. Carl Weber, 'Brecht as Director' (see above), p. 105.

10. ibid, p. 104.

5. Saint Joan of the Stockyards

1. Käthe Rülicke-Weiler, *Die Dramaturgie Brechts* (Berlin, 1968), 139–45.

2. *Die heilige Johanna der Schlachthöfe Programmheft des Berliner Ensembles* (Dec. 1967).

3. Review in *Hamburger Abendblatt*, 2.5.59.

4. Review in *Nürtinger Kreisnachrichten*, 6.5.59.

5. Review in *Hamburger Abendblatt*, 2.5.59.

6. Joachim Kaiser, in *Süddeutsche Zeitung*, 2.5.59.

7. Siegfried Melchinger, in *Stuttgarter Zeitung*, 5.5.59.

6. Mother Courage and her Children

1. The Methuen translation of 'kommt ein Sohn abhanden' as 'loses a son' (5ii, p. 3) does not bring out the oddity of the German phrase in this context.

2. Review in *Die neue Zeitung*, 15.1.49.

3. Review by Wolfgang Harich in *Tägliche Rundschau*, 14.1.49.

4. ibid.

5. Review in 'Der Sonntag', Berlin, 16.1.49.

6. Review in *Die Welt*, Hamburg, 15.1.49.

7. Jacques Callot (1592–1635), engraver and draughtsman, best known for the cycle 'Misères de la Guerre'.

7. The Life of Galileo

1. Werner Mittenzwei, *Bertolt Brecht, Von der 'Maßnahme' zu 'Leben des Galilei'* (Berlin, 1962), p. 274.

2. See Brecht, *Briefe*, ed. G. Glaeser (Frankfurt a.M., 1981), vol. 1, p. 387, p. 435.

3. *Stimme der Kritik*, Berlin-West, 17.1.57.

8. The Good Person of Szechwan

1. Walter Benjamin, *Versuche über Brecht* (Frankfurt a.M., 1967), p. 126.

2. Schumacher records the conversation with Brecht in his essay, 'Er wird bleiben', in Ernst Schumacher, *Brecht. Theater und Gesellschaft im 20. Jahrhundert* (Berlin, 1981), pp. 9–20.

3. Review in *Theater der Zeit*, Heft 12 (1957).

9. The Caucasian Chalk Circle

1. For an analysis of the emotive strategy employed in the 'Struggle for the Valley', see Peter Michelsen, ' "Und das Tal den Bewässerern . . ." über das Vorspiel zum Kaukasischen Kreidekreis', in *Drama und Theater im 20. Jahrhundert*, ed. H. D. Irmscher and W. Keller (Göttingen, 1983), pp. 190–203.

2. GW 15, p. 60.

3. *Brechts Theaterarbeit. Seine Inszenierung des 'Kaukasischen Kreidekreises' 1954*, ed. W. Hecht (Frankfurt a.M., 1985).

4. ibid, p. 197.
5. ibid, p. 199.
6. ibid, p. 168.
7. ibid, p. 206.
8. ibid, p. 202.
9. ibid, p. 198.

Bibliography

1. Brecht's works and related materials

Arbeitsjournal 1938–45, 3 vols, ed. W. Hecht (Frankfurt a.M., 1973).
Baal. Der böse Baal, der Asoziale, ed. D. Schmidt (Frankfurt a.M., 1968).
Baal. Drei Fassungen, ed. D. Schmidt (Frankfurt a.M., 1966).
Bertolt Brecht. Die heilige Johanna der Schlachthöfe. Bühnenfassung, Fragmente, Varianten, ed. G. Bahr (Frankfurt a.M., 1971).
Brechts 'Guter Mensch von Sezuan' (materials), ed. J. Knopf (Frankfurt a.M., 1982).
Brechts 'Kaukasischer Kreidekreis' (materials), ed. W. Hecht (Frankfurt a.M., 1985)
Brechts 'Leben des Galilei' (materials), ed. W. Hecht (Frankfurt a.M., 1981).
Brechts 'Mann ist Mann' (materials), ed. C. Wege (Frankfurt a.M., 1982).
Brechts 'Mutter Courage und ihre Kinder' (materials), ed. K. D. Müller (Frankfurt a.M., 1982).
Brechts Theaterarbeit. Seine Inszenierung des 'Kaukasischen Kreidekreises' 1954 (materials), ed. W. Hecht (Frankfurt a.M., 1985).
Brecht inszeniert. 'Der kaukasische Kreidekreis' (photos by G. Goedhart, text by A. Hurwicz) (Frankfurt a.M., 1964).
Bertolt Brecht on Stage (materials, photographs) (Frankfurt a.M., 1968).
Brecht on Theatre, ed. and trans. J. Willett (London, 1974).
Briefe, ed. G. Glaeser (Frankfurt a.M., 1981).

Collected Plays, Eyre Methuen edition, ed. J. Willett and R. Manheim (London, 1970 onwards).

Diaries 1920–1922, ed. H. Ramthun, trans J. Willett (London, 1979).

Gesammelte Werke, Suhrkamp edition, 20 vols (Frankfurt a.M., 1967).

Materialien zu Brechts 'Der kaukasische Kreidekreis', ed. W. Hecht (Frankfurt a.M., 1968).

Materialien zu Brechts 'Leben des Galilei', ed. W. Hecht (Frankfurt a.M., 1968).

Materialien zu Brechts 'Mutter Courage und ihre Kinder', ed. W. Hecht (Frankfurt a.M., 1967).

(The materials in these volumes are not identical with those in the more recent editions)

Poems, ed. J. Willett and R. Manheim (London, 1979).

Saint Joan of the Stockyards, trans. F. Jones (London, 1976).

Tagebücher 1920–1922. Autobiographische Aufzeichnungen 1920–54, ed. H. Ramthun (Frankfurt a.M., 1975).

The Messingkauf Dialogues, trans. J. Willett (London, 1964).

Trommeln in der Nacht (Munich, Drei Masken, 1922).

2. Biographical

Brecht as They Knew Him, ed. H. Witt, trans. J. Peet (London, 1975).

Brecht in Augsburg, ed. W. Frisch and K. W. Obermeier (Berlin, 1975).

A. Bronnen, *Tage mit Bertolt Brecht* (Munich, 1960).

M. Kesting, *Bertolt Brecht in Selbstzeugnissen und Bilddokumenten* (Hamburg, 1959).

J. K. Lyon, *Bertolt Brecht in America* (Princeton, 1980).

D. Pike, *German Writers in Soviet Exile* (Chapel Hill, 1982).

F. Sternberg, *der dichter und die ratio* (Göttingen, 1963).

K. Völker, *Brecht-Chronik* (Munich, 1971).

K. Völker, *Brecht: A Biography*, trans. J. Nowell (London, 1979).

3. Critical (mainly English)

E. Bentley, *The Brecht Commentaries 1943–80* (New York and London, 1981).

Bertolt Brecht: Political Theory and Literary Practice, ed. B. Weber and H. Heinen (Manchester, 1980).

Brecht in Perspective, ed. G. Bartram and A. Waine (London, 1982).

Brecht: A Collection of Critical Essays, ed. P. Demetz (Englewod Cliffs, N.J., 1962).

Bibliography

Brechts Dramen. Neue Interpretationen, ed. W. Hinderer (Stuttgart, 1984).

K. Dickson, *Towards Utopia: A Study of Brecht* (Oxford, 1978).

Essays on Brecht, ed. S. Mews and H. Knust (Chapel Hill, 1974).

M. Esslin, *Brecht. A Choice of Evils* (London, 1959).

F. Ewen, *Bertolt Brecht. His Life, his Art and his Times* (London, 1970).

R. Gray, *Brecht the Dramatist* (Cambridge, 1976).

R. Grimm, *Bertolt Brecht* (Stuttgart, 1971).

R. Grimm, *Bertolt Brecht. Die Struktur seines Werkes* (Nuremberg, 1959).

C. Hill, *Bertolt Brecht* (Boston, 1975).

W. Hinck, *Die Dramaturgie des späten Brecht* (Berlin, 1962).

W. Mittenzwei, *Von der 'Maßnahme' zu 'Leben des Galilei'* (Berlin, 1962).

M. Morley, *Brecht: A Study* (London, 1977).

J. Needle and P. Thomson, *Brecht* (Oxford, 1981).

D. Pike, *Lukács and Brecht* (Chapel Hill, 1985).

J. M. Ritchie, *Brecht, 'Der kaukasische Kreidekreis'* (London, 1976).

Sinn und Form. Zweites Sonderheft Bertolt Brecht (Berlin, 1957).

M. Spalter, *Brecht's Tradition* (Baltimore, 1967).

R. C. Speirs, *Brecht's Early Plays* (London, 1982).

A. Subiotto, *Bertolt Brecht's Adaptations for the Berliner Ensemble* (London, 1975).

A. White, *Bertolt Brecht's Great Plays* (London, 1978).

J. Willett, *The Theatre of Bertolt Brecht. A Study from Eight Aspects* (London, 1959).

J. Willett, *Brecht in Context. Comparative Approaches* (London, 1984).

4. Collected Reviews

In addition to the following items, a number of the 'materials' volumes contain reviews of productions.

H. Jhering, *Von Reinhardt bis Brecht*, 3 vols (Berlin, 1958–61).

G. Rühle, *Theater für die Republik* (Frankfurt a.M., 1967).

E. Schumacher, *Brecht-Kritiken* (Berlin, 1977).

M. Wyss, *Brecht in der Kritik* (Munich, 1977).

Index

Index

Index

Index

Index